Trans and Autistic

of related interest

Gender Identity, Sexuality and Autism
Voices from Across the Spectrum
Eva Mendes and Meredith R. Maroney
ISBN 978 1 78592 754 6
eISBN 978 1 78450 585 1

Uncomfortable Labels
My Life as a Gay Autistic Trans Woman
Laura Kate Dale
ISBN 978 1 78592 587 0
eISBN 978 1 78592 588 7

Transitioning Together
One Couple's Journey of Gender and Identity Discovery
Wenn B. Lawson and Beatrice M. Lawson
ISBN 978 1 78592 103 2
eISBN 978 1 78450 365 9

The Autism Spectrum Guide to Sexuality and Relationships
Understand Yourself and Make Choices that are Right for You
Dr Emma Goodall
Forewords by Dr Wenn Lawson and Jeanette Purkis
ISBN 978 1 84905 705 9
eISBN 978 1 78450 226 3

TRANS AND AUTISTIC

Stories from Life at the Intersection

NOAH ADAMS
and
BRIDGET LIANG

Jessica Kingsley Publishers
London and Philadelphia

First published in 2020
by Jessica Kingsley Publishers
73 Collier Street
London N1 9BE, UK
and
400 Market Street, Suite 400
Philadelphia, PA 19106, USA

www.jkp.com

Library of Congress Cataloging in Publication Data
A CIP catalog record for this book is available from the Library of Congress

British Library Cataloguing in Publication Data
A CIP catalogue record for this book is available from the British Library

ISBN 978 1 78592 484 2
eISBN 978 1 78450 875 3

Printed and bound in the United States of America by LSC Communications

BRIDGET'S THANKS

Thanks to my chosen fam and community. I wouldn't be alive today if I didn't have people who supported me. I wouldn't have found the autistic trans community without them either. This book is the product of our desires for a world where we can exist as autistic and trans folks. I thank the folks from my communities who volunteered to be interviewed. Our movement will grow and, I hope, we'll all be treated as fully fledged human beings someday soon.

NOAH'S THANKS

This book would never have been possible without the help and support of my family, friends, and community. First of all, thank you to my wonderful fiancée Katherine, who provided a steady hand and excellent copyediting throughout. Thank you to Reubs Walsh, who helped with designing this book and conducting interviews. Thank you to Paul McFadden, without whom I might still be fretting about how to start. To Dani Castro, for influencing the way participants were recruited. And especially to all those who shared their stories with us: Alex, Grace, Isabella, James, Moose, Nami, Nathan, Reynard, Sherry, and Tristan.

Contents

Glossary

Some of the terms in the following pages will be familiar to you. Some will not. We've included this glossary to provide common definitions for terms in use by and important to the communities we talk about. They are up to date at the time of publication.

The language used by the transgender community is rapidly evolving and some terms may have alternate or even completely different meanings within a short period of time.[1] As a result, it is likely, and perhaps inevitable, that they may seem woefully out of date by the time you read this. Other terms currently mean different things to different people and in different cultural and geographical contexts. For instance, in Brazil and many parts of South America, travesti (translated from Portuguese as transvestite) is a reclaimed and preferred term for many people who were assigned male at birth and express a feminine gender identity.[2] In most parts of North America and Europe, however, it would be offensive. As a result, you should take this glossary as advisory and always ask what the individuals and communities you interact with prefer to be called, and follow their lead when they tell you.

ABA: Applied behavioural therapy. The most commonly researched "treatment" for autism. Its goal is to modify autistic behaviours to be indistinguishable from neurotypicals'. It is highly controversial and widely decried by the autism community.

Allistic: Non-autistic.

Asexual: Not having sexual feelings for others. Individuals who are asexual may still have romantic feelings.

Chosen family: Often used to draw a line between a person's biological family, from which they may have experienced rejection, and the people that they have chosen, and who have chosen them, to be in a family with.

Cisgender: Not transgender. A person whose gender assigned at birth and their current understanding of their gender identity match.

Greysexual: Closely related to asexual. Differs to the extent that the person may occasionally, or in specific circumstances, experience sexual attraction.

Head canon: The personal reinterpretation, by a fan, of a specific media property (e.g. *Steven Universe*). This may include, for example, reinterpreting the backstory to render a character transgender or autistic. It contrasts with canon, which is the explicitly portrayed version of the property by its creators.

Identify-first vs. person-first language: We use both identity-first (e.g. autistic person) and person-first (e.g. person with autism) language in this book according to individual participants' preference. There is, however, a great deal of argument within the autistic community as to which is preferable, reflecting a wider debate in the disability community.[3] Though no consensus exists, and the ultimate choice is each individual's, there is general preference within the autistic community towards identity-first language, because it is seen as accepting and even celebrating "autism as an inherent part of an individual's identity."[4] By contrast, person-first language is typically used by parents and professionals to humanize the person and, perhaps subconsciously, divorce them from what may be seen as negative aspects of being autistic.

Neurotypical: Closely related to allistic but differs to the extent that it encompasses people who do not have attention deficit hyperactivity disorder (ADHD), dyslexia, or other neurological conditions.

Pansexual: People who have no sexual preference with regards to sex assigned at birth or gender identity.

Trans broken arm syndrome: The tendency of healthcare professionals to blame unrelated medical ailments on one's transgender status.[5,6] For instance, a person attends an emergency room department for a broken limb and, on finding out their trans status, is asked by medical professionals whether the two are connected. More onerously, those who have undergone gender-confirming surgeries have also been asked to display their genitals to curious doctors and their students.[7,8]

Transgender: A person who experiences a different gender identity than the one they were assigned at birth. We have intentionally used the term transgender, rather than trans or trans*, throughout this text.

Transmisogyny: In its simplest form, hatred of transgender women, either explicitly, or subtly. The latter may take the form of portraying transgender women as weak and encouraging violence against them.

Transsexual: Closely related to transgender, which is the umbrella term, but denotes an intention to pursue surgical interventions to align one's gender identity with one's body and may imply binary (e.g. male/female) gender.

ENDNOTES

1   Bouman *et al.*, 2017
2   Campuzano, 2006
3   Fletcher-Watson, 2016
4   Brown, 2011
5   Knutson *et al.*, 2016
6   Payton, 2015
7   Chisolm-Straker *et al.*, 2017
8   Brown, 2011

INTRODUCTION

NIHIL DE NOBIS, SINE NOBIS[1]

We wrote this book because we've noticed that while there is an increasing amount of research on the subject of gender identity and autism, there is distressingly little from the perspective of transgender and autistic people themselves. We argue, as transgender and autistic academics, for an approach that takes into account our viewpoints in the creation of this research[2] and we assert that, as the title of this section suggests, nothing should be created about us, without us.[3]

We wrote this book for other transgender and autistic people, and the researchers and clinicians with whom we interact. We hope that other autistic and/or transgender people will see themselves and their experiences mirrored here. We also hope that non-autistic researchers and clinical practitioners will read these stories, learn about this population's diversity and capability, and consider this when they interact with and study us. After all, "If you've met one person with autism, you've met one person with autism."[4] Contrary to this, much of the clinical and research training on this subject focuses on their supposed homogeneity and, where transitional healthcare is desired, the need for extended assessment and gatekeeping procedures.

In fact, there is a long history of research that exploits us as marginalized populations, with the goal of producing knowledge that benefits the researcher, while far too often being at best irrelevant or at worst actively harmful to members of the populations themselves.[5,6] Conventional research on this subject focuses on the supposed need for special assessment protocols and longer waiting periods to access transitional care for autistics, at odds with the stated goals of many of our participants.[7] Our participants, far from seeing or receiving this as helpful, respond by choosing not to disclose their autism, avoiding healthcare, and circumventing this gatekeeping in a myriad of ways. Indeed, individuals have been outright denied hormones due to autism, sometimes with tragic results. One such example is Kayden Clarke, who was killed by police during a mental health crisis after his doctor told him she wouldn't "prescribe testosterone until his Asperger's was cured."[8]

By contrast, many autistics, and most of our participants, view both their autism and transgender identity as an intrinsic and naturally occurring part of themselves that, even if it were possible, they would not change. Within this context, it is abusive to subject us to longer waiting periods to access transitional care; rather than reducing harm, such policies only encourage us to hide parts of ourselves and/or find alternative means to access what we need.

Our book challenges this conventional perspective and explores issues that matter to individual transgender and autistic people. We shine a light, in particular, on their experiences with self-discovery, healthcare, and family and community support. Unfortunately, and largely due to stigma and discrimination, these experiences are often negative or at least fraught. The majority, for instance, experienced (or self-censored for fear of experiencing) denial of transitional healthcare due to autism. On the flip side, many experienced various barriers around obtaining autistic services, most notably a diagnosis, often because they were told they "didn't seem autistic."

Conversely, no one individual had a simple or straightforward experience of discovering themselves to be, and articulating themselves as, transgender and/or autistic. While many of their difficulties in this regard mirrored conventional transitional narratives, several related directly to their autism. For instance, while all felt that both autistic and transgender aspects of their identity were inherent and immutable, several discussed how autism made it more difficult to determine what neurotypical people meant by gender identity, and how to articulate their own in a way that was legible to them.

Several participants had conditional, limited, or no family support. For some, this meant a strong relationship with one parent and none with the other, or strong relationships with siblings and not parents. Other participants no longer had a relationship with any family, and several, though not a majority, relayed stories of physically and emotionally abusive childhoods. For most, family rejection was attributable to their transgender identity rather than autism. In the present, most if not all participants had formed tightly knit communities and "chosen families," and many were very involved, as both participants and activists, in the transgender and/or autistic communities.

We recognize that healthcare providers and researchers are struggling to achieve a baseline of knowledge on what may appear to be a new and emerging population of transgender and autistic individuals. Too often, however, they fail to consult with autistic and transgender people, or consider that the people in front of them may differ from case studies. Likewise, the issues that appeal to these professionals may have little or no relationship with those that are important to transgender and autistic people.

Many professionals, for instance, desire to know the number of transgender people that are autistic, or vice versa, which has little import to people struggling to access basic healthcare. In any case, while there are a growing number of reports discussing the potential overlap between transgender and autistic experiences, it also isn't possible to say whether this is the result of something inherent to transgender or autistic people.[9,10,11] It may, for instance, be that transgender people are more likely to be diagnosed with autism because they are subject to a greater deal of assessment and diagnosis than others. If this is true, the rate of autism among transgender individuals will increase alongside academic calls to routinely screen them for autism.[12] Another complicating factor is that a diagnosis of autism relies on impairment in social situations, an area in which transgender people may be uniquely weak, or avoidant of, due to discrimination and prejudice.[13]

Nevertheless, transgender and autistic people clearly exist—if not by virtue of the many support and self-advocacy groups, then demonstrated by the existence of this book and its authors. We provide an introduction to the issues that matter to this group, and explore their strength, resourcefulness, and tenacity in pursuing them against all odds. One Japanese man, for instance, escaped abuse at home and ultimately pursued transition by seeking out global educational scholarships while barely a teen. Others made similar leaps from familiar homes and cultures to an uncertain but hopeful future. Most formed strong and lasting relationships within the transgender and, in some cases, autistic communities—often also becoming activists and advocates for these causes. Another young man established a career as a researcher in a transgender health laboratory, and one woman even ran for political office.

The individuals interviewed in these pages have clearly achieved a great deal, in some cases in spite of incredible discrimination, and always as a result of the unique perspective and worldview afforded to them by their autism and transgender identity. These conversations and the stories that we produced together are, however, only a beginning. We hope that they will increase the attention paid to the diversity and lived experiences of people who are both transgender and autistic.

PARTICIPANT SELECTION

Participants were selected through an intentional process, which prioritized the recruitment of as diverse a group as possible, particularly with regards to ethnicity and gender identity. We achieved this through a multi-stage process. We first posted a call for participants on a private Facebook group for attendees of a yearly transgender and autistic workshop facilitated by the first author. We then screened respondents in order to ensure diversity. Finally, we asked individuals who had been interviewed to recommend others whom they both thought might be interested and would represent a typically under-represented group. We supplemented this through our own personal and professional networks. We checked in throughout this process to ensure that we had interviewed a wide range of individuals and made necessary course corrections in order to do so.

In the end, we talked to a diverse group of ten individuals who identified, broadly, as both transgender and autistic. While we've edited and curated these interviews for each chapter, we've also strained to keep them as authentic to the individual voices as possible. Accordingly, each person interviewed has received a copy of the final chapter for approval.

DATA COLLECTION

As noted, we collected data primarily through an open-ended interview instrument, which we developed for this purpose (see Appendix 2). This allowed us to engage participants in a discussion around core issues, while not limiting their responses, or the direction of the conversation, to these topics. More importantly, as there is a history of research exploitation in this population,[14] our questions allowed us to ethically and authentically represent our participants' stories. We also developed and applied a short, 11-item questionnaire (see Appendix 3), which allowed us to gather basic demographic data, such as gender identity, pronouns, sexual orientation, income, and information about their autism diagnosis. We compared this data in order to present a baseline snapshot of our participants' location.

Interviews were conducted by the authors and Reubs Walsh, a transgender and autistic doctoral candidate who is resident in Amsterdam. They took place between April 2018 and March 2019 and ranged from one to almost seven hours, over one to two sessions. All participants were provided an honorarium of $100 Canadian in respect of their time and expertise. The open-ended interview focused on everything from when participants first knew they were autistic, to their perception of representation of transgender/autistic experiences in popular media. While not a question, over the course of the interviews, nine of the ten participants discussed their experiences with work. This shouldn't be surprising, as evidence suggests that autistic people experience a number of employment barriers.[15,16,17] We have, as a result, discussed the employment experiences of those who addressed it.

Participants were offered the choice to complete the interview via text messenger, Skype, in person, by phone, or another method of their devising. Seven opted to be interviewed via text (Facebook/Skype messenger), two by video (Facebook/Skype), and only one in person. Recorded interviews were transcribed and analyzed, together with text-based interviews, using Dedoose, which is a mixed-methods research platform. Autistic symptomatology was usually cited as the reason for selecting an online and, in particular, text interview, with concerns about becoming non-verbal and/or needing time to process questions being paramount to this decision. Interestingly, there is emerging research which suggests that text-based interviewing is indeed a more accessible interview methodology for autistic people.[18,19] Of course, the location of the interviewee was also a consideration, as the interviewers were located in Toronto and Amsterdam, while participants were in the USA (n=5), Canada (n=4), and the UK (n=1).

CONSENT

All participants signed an informed consent form (see Appendix 1) that explained our study, detailed its risks and benefits, and requested consent for the following: participation in the study as a whole; the interview (if in person or by voice) to be audio recorded; the inclusion of comments and quotes in this book; and, if they choose, to be de-anonymized in it. We provided the latter option because the majority (six out of ten) of participants felt strongly about attaching their name to their story. We were able to respect this in all cases but one, where the participant chose to be identifiable, but we opted to obfuscate their identity due to their irregular immigration status. The remaining three participants selected their own pseudonym.

DEMOGRAPHIC FINDINGS

Participants ranged in age from 21 to 36 years old, averaging 29. Seven were formally diagnosed as autistic, and the remaining three were self-diagnosed. Six identified their diagnosis as autism, two Asperger's, and the other two didn't feel able to say, lacking a formal diagnosis. They use a wide range of pronouns, with gender identities including, broadly, five primarily transfeminine, four primarily transmasculine, and three primarily genderqueer, non-binary, or agender. These three identity categories weren't otherwise mutually exclusive. Participants' assigned sex at birth was male in four cases, female in five, with one declining to answer. All ten identified as queer in an umbrella sense, with many selecting additional identities of asexual, bisexual, pansexual, gay, heterosexual, greysexual, lesbian, and homoromantic. While this was undoubtedly influenced by our recruitment strategies, there is evidence that autistic people are much more likely to be non-heterosexual.[20,21]

Three were born in Canada, three in the USA, and one in each of Germany, Japan, Taiwan, and the UK. Participants also represented an array of racial and ethnic identities. Five were white (two of whom were Jewish), three Asian, and two Black/African American. Three also explicitly identified as bi/multiracial. In total, ethnic/racial identities included Afro-Caribbean, Black, British/English, Canadian, Caucasian, Chinese, German, Han Chinese, Irish, Japanese, Jewish, Korean, Lithuanian Jew, Native, Slovenian, Taiwanese Hakka, and Vietnamese. This was more diverse than other samples, though ours was clearly not randomly selected, as diversity was a central focus of recruitment.[22]

Yearly incomes, standardized to USD, ranged from $0 to $67,498.40, with an average of $18,218.19. Three participants made less than $5,000; one made $5–10,000; four made $10–20,000; one made $20–40,000; and one made more than $50,000. This is consistent with research findings of low income among transgender respondents.[23,24] Research on the subject of earning and income among autistic adults is muddied by the field's focus on parents and lack of services and support for adults. However, there is emerging evidence that these individuals are underemployed,[25] and that, where appropriate support is provided, employment increases dramatically.[26] This would suggest that our findings of low income are unsurprising.

Regarding the highest level of education achieved, two participants achieved some college/trade school; one graduated college/trade school; five have some university education; one completed a bachelor's degree; and two achieved a university graduate or professional degree. This method of categorization, typically used in a census, was complicated by one participant who obtained both some college or trade school and some university education. It also reflects the fact that the "some university" includes both people who are currently in school and those who have been forced by circumstance to cease their studies. Regarding transgender participants, education is often complicated and disrupted by discrimination from peers and educators, resulting in stunted or late educational development.[27,28] There is little research on educational attainment among autistic adults, though that among children emphasizes the potential for academic success when given necessary supports.[29]

These are the bare facts. They don't give you an idea of who the people we talked to are, or what they think about the world and their place in it. In the following pages and chapters, you will get a chance to know them, in their own words. We hope that it provides insight into the lived experiences of people who are both transgender and autistic. It would be trite, and too easy, to say that we are just like everyone else, as this is both a true statement and one that is completely inadequate. We are individuals, like everyone else, which makes all of us wholly unique, and totally unpredictable.

ENDNOTES

1   Nothing about us without us, in the original Latin. Please see page 135 for more information.
2   Adams *et al.*, 2017
3   Pellicano, 2018
4   Lime Connect, 2018
5   Tagonist, 2009
6   Smith, 1999
7   Strang *et al.*, 2018a
8   Ellis, 2016
9   Strang *et al.*, 2018b
10   Nobili *et al.*, 2018
11   White, 2016

12 Janssen, Huang, & Duncan, 2016
13 Jacobs *et al.*, 2014
14 Adams *et al.*, 2017
15 Sarrett, 2017
16 Lorenz *et al.*, 2016
17 Standifer, 2011a,b
18 Benford & Standen, 2011
19 Nicolaidis *et al.*, 2019
20 George & Stokes, 2018
21 Strang, 2018
22 The Williams Institute, 2016
23 Bauer & Scheim, 2015
24 Grant *et al.*, 2011
25 Hendricks, 2010
26 Howlin, Alcock, & Burkin, 2005
27 The Williams Institute, 2018
28 James *et al.*, 2016
29 Keen, Webster, & Ridley, 2016

ALEX

Born in Toronto, to white South African immigrants of Lithuanian-Jewish descent, Alex is a 21-year-old autistic self-advocate who identifies as queer, genderfluid, and non-binary. They are currently a student at Seneca College working towards a diploma in social service work. Diagnosed with Asperger's syndrome when they were just under six years old, they only found out several years later. Alex came out as transgender towards the end of high school and is now very involved in the queer and autistic communities. They use a range of pronouns and, for this chapter, will be using they/them. Alex is their real name.

COMING OUT AS AUTISTIC

Alex was diagnosed with Asperger's syndrome on the first day of elementary school, five days before their sixth birthday. However, they weren't aware of this fact until almost three years later, when they were placed in a special education classroom for children with autism. Alex recalls being frustrated by the large gap of time between first receiving a diagnosis and being made aware of it. They had already known from a young age that they weren't like their peers and, lacking an explanation for these differences, tended to blame themselves for their social difficulties. Alex had particular difficulty understanding why they interacted with their peers differently from the perceived norm, struggled to make and maintain friendships, and were prone to violent meltdowns. In this context, being told they were autistic was a huge relief that helped them to better understand themselves and the way in which they are unique.

On being informed of their diagnosis with Asperger's syndrome, and to help foster their newfound sense of identity as an autistic person, Alex was given the book *Asperger's Huh?*[1] This book was extremely helpful to them, first in providing evidence that their experiences were shared by other people, which they found comforting, then in helping them to finally relate to their peers by giving them a language to describe their experiences. For several years, they even referred to their hyperfixations as "weebies," which is a term used by a character in the book to describe their special interest in the weather. Alex also often lent the book to friends as a quick and easy way to explain their disability. Unfortunately, this ultimately resulted in it being lost and, as a result, they had to learn to define and describe themselves without it.

Autism has become a major part of Alex's identity by giving them a sense of belonging with other autistic people and culture. Ultimately, they have come to see themselves as part of the larger neurodiversity community, which has influenced and defined many aspects of their life. This has, in turn, shaped the manner in which they choose to socialize. Alex recalls, for instance, that when they were younger they often introduced themselves to new people by proactively disclosing their diagnoses. Prior to this expression of pride and radical self-acceptance, however, they had tended to take out their internalized ableism on more visibly autistic classmates. Alex explains that this attitude was at least partially influenced by applied behavioural analysis (ABA), the principles of which influenced their treatment as a youth. As an adult, they had to deliberately unlearn many of the lessons taught by ABA in order to fully appreciate their authentic autistic self. Alex now socializes almost exclusively with other disabled people due, in part, to being exhausted by ableism.

As a radical autistic and queer advocate, who has been identified as such in several media interviews, Alex is very open and outspoken about their identity. As result, they don't often find themselves in a position where they need to disclose their disability and, in fact, don't necessarily have the option not to. However, this is a choice Alex has made consciously and, in some ways, being so open about their disability helps to avoid being placed in a situation where ableism might cause an issue. They realized, shortly after being informed of their diagnosis, that this disclosure helped others to understand them better. However, Alex has found that some of their peers act patronizingly and condescendingly after finding out this information. Still, whenever they are in the company of someone new and feel the need to disclose, they make a point of doing so. While Alex believes strongly in the individual's right to choose whether to disclose, they also feel that a person's initial reactions to disclosure can be a good barometer for whether they should continue to interact.

COMING OUT AS TRANSGENDER

Alex was assigned male at birth but, in many ways, always knew they didn't identify as male. However, they didn't realize until later in life that they didn't necessarily have to. They explained that masculinity wasn't something that was aggressively forced on them so much as that they were passively obligated to accept it, simply because they didn't know they could question it. As a genderfluid person who fluctuates between identifying as agender, non-binary, and transfeminine, Alex sees the entire concept of gender as something that is "elusive, aloof, rigid, and often unappealing, yet somehow still deeply alluring, enigmatic, dynamic, and even magical."

Alex recalled having difficulty relating to their male peers as early as kindergarten. However, they also weren't particularly interested in seeing themselves as "one of the boys" to begin with. Alex usually felt the greatest sense of belonging among their female friends. Alex didn't have a chance to actively explore their gender identity until around the age of 13, when they started playing the massively multiplayer online role-playing games (MMORPGs) *Clone Wars Adventures*[2] and *Star Wars: The Old Republic*.[3] These games gave them the opportunity to experiment by using female characters and taking on feminine personas. Alex didn't initially realize that their gravitation towards female characters might not be a typical cisgender experience, having rationalized that "every boy wants to be a girl sometimes." However, this turned out to be a pivotal experience in helping Alex to discover their queer identities.

Another pivotal moment in helping Alex to understand their gender identity was when one of their friends, who is also on the autism spectrum, came out as transgender. This act helped them to understand that there is language to describe their experience. This realization led Alex to learn about the common overlap between queerness and autism through personal blogs and academic studies. They subsequently came out as queer, became a member of their school's gender and sexuality alliance, and joined several Facebook groups for people who are queer, and/or autistic, which gave them a sense of belonging to a huge online community.

LINKS BETWEEN AUTISM AND GENDER IDENTITY

While acknowledging that other people's experiences are different, Alex feels strongly that their own autism and transgender identity are interlinked. They've also noticed that many of their autistic friends are queer and vice versa and that several of them feel that their transgender and autistic experiences are connected. Alex posits that this may be due to autistic people's tendency to be non-conforming, open to new ideas, and the proliferation of community spaces for transgender/autistic people.

However, Alex also feels that, unlike autism, assigned binary sex is a very flimsy social construct based on arbitrarily gendered physical traits that don't necessarily reflect people's genetics; some cis women, for instance, have XY chromosomes. They are also quite aware of the contradictions in gender role expectations which, because they make little objective sense, they fail to see the need to conform to. Alex does, however, acknowledge that this reaction may be influenced by their autistic nature to pick apart and question everything. In this context, gender could be seen as a part of neurotypical culture that is often inscrutable and inapplicable to many autistic people. One could also conclude that autistic people, by their very nature, expose the lies in universal or fixed gender identity.

Alex discusses how being autistic can make coming to terms with your gender identity more difficult. Their own experience of autism made it difficult to identify the language to describe their experience. As a result, Alex accepted the name and pronouns given to them as inevitable, if imperfect, and didn't automatically connect this to a transgender experience until another friend transitioned and offered an example that they could apply to themselves.

In Alex's case, being autistic has also made identifying the level of transitional healthcare they wish to pursue more difficult. At present, they are focused on identifying their gender identity and determining what this means for their particular transitional pathway, as distinct from that expected of other transgender people, particularly with regards to medical transition. This is complicated by Alex's non-binary gender identity and the tendency of healthcare practitioners to, in their words, give minimal information about transitional options to this group. Finally, as Alex notes, autistic people—especially those who aren't labelled as high functioning—can be seen to lack the capacity to make decisions regarding transition. As they suggest, these difficulties may also be related to autistic people's tendency to pick apart and question everything and, by that token, attempt to plan for every eventuality. In Alex's case, executive dysfunction can occur when this doesn't happen.

FAMILY

Alex has several family members who, like them, have a variety of disabilities, including anxiety, ADHD, depression, and autism. They describe their family as particularly supportive of their autism. Growing up in an affluent household and neighbourhood, Alex had access to resources not necessarily available to others and has, overall, benefitted from a supportive community. Their parents, for instance, had the capacity to advocate for them at school. Alex is also able to live at home where their nanny, whom the family has employed since they were four years old, prepares their meals and does their laundry. This has allowed them to excel academically in high school and gain admittance to college.

However, though their parents advocated for their involvement, Alex has consistently been excluded from healthcare and educational decision making. This has, in many ways, deprived them of the opportunity to develop life skills that they are only now learning in the midst of college. Alex's grades have suffered as a result, which led to a depressive episode and, in turn, more difficulties in school. Making doctor's appointments and managing medical care have been particularly stressful, and they struggle not to rely on their parents for help managing these situations. Alex identifies a recent visit to get tested for sexually transmitted infections as one of the first times they'd independently managed a medical appointment, which they found frightening but also empowering.

Alex describes their parents as supportive, though they sometimes struggle to understand that Alex's abilities and needs fluctuate and have become more complex with age. For instance, though usually very verbal, Alex sometimes struggles with communicating during increased stress, impacting their ability to use full sentences without stuttering, and occasionally being unable to talk at all. In these instances, Alex sometimes relies on their iPhone to communicate through text. They have also explored using American Sign Language to communicate while non-verbal, as they find this somewhat easier than using text. Unfortunately, Alex has found that many people in their life are unable or unwilling to learn at least its basics. Still, they are thankful for their father's wisdom and the many candid conversations they've had together, as well as their mother's dedication to her advocacy work with the autism community.

Alex's family initially struggled to understand what it meant for them to identify as a transfeminine, non-binary, and gender non-conforming woman and, for instance, initially expressed confusion that they didn't change their wardrobe after coming out. However, over time they have become much more understanding and supportive. For instance, Alex shares one occasion where their father relayed a relative's message of being proud of them "for being who they are and not letting other people dictate how they live their life." This message came not long after a Rosh Hashanah dinner during which Alex chose to wear a feminine outfit for the first time in front of their extended family. Alex's parents were particularly supportive of this, even warning an unsupportive family member not to say anything and agreeing to ask him to leave if he did.

COMMUNITY AND ACTIVISM

Alex is very involved in the queer and disabled communities and chooses to socialize almost exclusively within them. As an adolescent, Alex spent their summers at an overnight camp for neurodivergent children.[4] Alex credits this experience, alongside other autistic community spaces, with helping them to accept themselves as queer, disabled, and neurodivergent, and serving as one source of inspiration to persue social service work. More recently, while in their first year of college, they took part in the inaugural meeting of Autistiqueers,[5] which provides peer support to queer autistic people in Toronto. Alex later co-founded and served on the executive committee of Autistics For Autistics,[6] a grassroots organization that advocates for governmental reform in the creation of autism policy and services. They stepped down from this position after they were invited to join the Centre for Addiction and Mental Health's[7] youth advisory group as its first autistic member. Soon after, they were appointed to serve on the Ontario Autism Program[8] advisory panel, another historic first for autistic Ontarians.

As noted, Alex's involvement in the autism community and in embracing autistic culture has meant they have had to unlearn the tendency to mask their autistic traits, taught to them through ABA, which was developed to make autistic children appear "normal" through repetitive behavioural trials. It is the most widely practiced therapy for autism and just as widely derided as abusive by the autistic community for both the manner in which it is conducted and its focus on suppressing inherent traits.[9] Alex found the manipulative aspect of this therapy abusive, while they acknowledge that those interventions, offered with their full knowledge and consent, could have been helpful. In any case, many of the strategies learned in these sessions, such as sustained eye contact, have been unhelpful and even detrimental to Alex's interactions with other autistic people. In this sense, Alex suggests that there are a number of parallels between autistic and Deaf culture, though they are careful to point out that the experiences aren't identical.[10] Nevertheless, they have found themselves to be happier and much more comfortable within the autistic community.

Though they didn't know him personally, Alex also attended the same high school and was in the same special education class as Alek Minassian, who perpetrated the Toronto van attack.[11] Alex condemns his actions, but also found the characterization of him as incapable of driving or uniquely prone to violence due to autism infuriating. Thanks to their position as an autistic advocate and connections to other figures in the community, Alex was contacted by the *Toronto Star* to offer insight into this case.[12] In discussing this, they posited that Minassian, and other socially isolated young autistic men like him, might be particularly vulnerable to the radicalizing ideology that proliferates on online forums like Reddit and 4chan. The lack of comprehensive social and sexual education for disabled people might also create an environment in which people with incel[13] ideology can prey on these young men. Alex fears for the stigma that could be cast on other autistic people by Minassian's actions.

RELIGION

Alex derives a lot of support from their cultural, religious, and ethnic heritage as a Lithuanian Jew, a community they describe as tightknit. They ascribe their propensity to think critically and question everything, in part, to the fact that this trait is taught and prized in the Jewish community. Alex takes inspiration from the knowledge that the Talmud has historically been inclusive of a multitude of gender identities. These include Zachar (male), Nekeivah (female), Androgynos (both male and female characteristics), Tumtum (indeterminate), Ay'lonit (female at birth, develops male characteristics at puberty, and/or is infertile), and Saris (male at birth, develops female characteristics at puberty, and/or is castrated).[14,15] Alex also related the story of 14th-century Provençal rabbi, Kalonymus ben Kalonymus, who wrote a book of poetry, known as the *Even Bochan*,[16] in which he expressed wishing to have been a woman.[17] They find it amusing that their religious name, Kalman, is a Yiddish diminutive of Kalonymus.

Alex describes some especially moving instances in which their rabbi provided emotional and spiritual support. In particular, they recall receiving a warm hug from their rabbi in response to coming out to them. On another occasion, Alex received a voicemail expressing the rabbi's pride in them for attending their first pride parade and thankfulness that people no longer have to hide their sexual and gender identities. Still, they don't always find the Jewish world so accepting, and characterized some of the leadership of their local synagogue as racist and queerphobic. Though Alex attended a Hasidic congregation for most of their lives, they haven't felt safe enough to continue doing so since 2018. The last time they entered their childhood synagogue was when they took part in a mikveh[18] ceremony created for transgender Jews on the day they started hormone replacement therapy.

WORK

Alex is working towards their diploma in social service work as a student at Seneca College. They hope to obtain a bachelor's degree in this field and ultimately practice as a social worker, where they plan to act as a role model for other autistic people, especially youth. Alex credits their rabbi, who is neurodivergent, as having been a major source of inspiration in their decision to go into the helping profession. They currently volunteer at the York Federation of Students Access Centre and volunteered previously as a camp counsellor at Camp Kennebec. Alex also worked as a camp counsellor for Autism Ontario.

HEALTHCARE

Alex has had a mixed experience with healthcare. On the one hand, they credit early autism diagnosis and placement in supportive learning environments as very helpful. They have a good relationship with their cognitive behavioural therapy practitioner, whose support was crucial to accessing academic accommodations, especially for test-taking. They also had a very good relationship with their pediatrician, who they stayed with as long as possible before switching over to an adult physician. Alex has found this transition to be more difficult than they expected it would be.

On the other hand, Alex has had a number of problematic healthcare experiences, particularly around neuropsychiatric diagnoses. Several years after receiving a diagnosis of autism they were misdiagnosed with oppositional defiant disorder (ODD) around the same time they received diagnoses of ADHD, generalized anxiety disorder, and a learning disability. Fortunately, Alex's parents were firm that the ODD label was incorrect and it was never affirmed in another assessment. In relation to the psycho-educational evaluation they took before entering college, Alex opines that these assessments assume that people know to answer questions "as if it's their worst day," which may not be obvious to those with autism or who are unfamiliar with the process.

Alex currently takes medication for ADHD, anxiety, and depression. They were also referred to an endocrinologist when they were 13 or 14 years old, who prescribed Lupron to correct slow development of height. Alex described the experience of seeing the endocrinologist as deeply uncomfortable, not just because they were unfamiliar with them, but also because the visits involved genital examinations. They also found visits to the dentist difficult due to anxiety and autism-related sensory issues.

As mentioned, Alex is very critical of ABA, which they characterize as relying on a "hidden curriculum" that denied their intelligence and capability, manipulated them into participating, and lacked informed consent. As they noted, these interventions have also been linked to post-traumatic stress disorder[19] and, indeed, they struggle with internalized ableism and stereotypes about the limited potential of autistic people. In contrast, Alex looks back fondly on play therapy, which was characterized by open communication, trust, and emphasis on their needs and wants. Unfortunately, ABA is often the only autism treatment that receives government funding in many jurisdictions.

Alex also worries about suicidality in the autistic community. Certainly, there is evidence that suicide, attributed partially to depression and abuse, is increased in this population.[20,21] This would suggest that transgender people, who are already at high risk of suicidality, are particularly impacted.[22] Alex has known a number of autistic people, including themselves, who have experienced suicidality.

When Alex was in grade three, they frequently experienced physical restraint in a traumatizing manner. This led to their expulsion and subsequently to becoming suicidal. Alex relates this trauma, and their experiences of emotional abuse in past relationships, to undermining their bodily autonomy. By contrast, they feel that this might have been avoided had they received comprehensive, autism-centric education on sexual health and consent from an early age.[23]

Alex's experience with transgender healthcare has been decidedly fraught, as they struggle to separate what healthcare interventions they want from what is expected of them by other transgender people, their parents, and healthcare practitioners (who may not be familiar with non-binary options). They worry that they may end up medically transitioning for the sake of other people's perceptions of what a woman should look like. Alex is not, however, overly concerned that healthcare practitioners may deny them treatment because they are autistic, though they worry that some of the trappings of autism, like executive dysfunction, may interfere with their ability to navigate these systems, or that their autism might be blamed for unrelated things (e.g. autistic broken arm syndrome). More generally, they express concern that their other mental health issues, like ADHD, depression, and dissociation, might cause practitioners to hesitate. Despite these concerns, they are currently receiving hormone replacement therapy.

MEDIA REPRESENTATION

Alex has seen some popular media representation of autistic people (e.g. *Atypical*,[24] *The Big Bang Theory*,[25] *The Good Doctor*[26]), but other than a biopic about Temple Grandin,[27] hasn't found it to be particularly accurate or helpful. They can't think of any popular media representation of people who are both transgender and autistic, and the only positive transgender representation they mentioned was *Steven Universe*,[28] which features transgender and neurodivergent representation, and has a non-binary, Jewish creator. Interestingly, Alex didn't characterize the absence of media as entirely negative, due to the tendency of cisgender, heterosexual, and allistic[29] people to take any representation as universal (e.g. *Rain Man*[30]). In fact, they have often been compared to Sheldon from *The Big Bang Theory*, which they find offensive, given the character's selfish personality traits.

SOCIAL RULES

Alex has difficulty with social rules, particularly as they relate to social expectations of males, females, and those who are non-binary. They recognize that, where they live, the expectation is that non-binary people stereotypically present in a particular way (e.g. flat chest, multicoloured hair shaved on one side, or an undercut). However, this is not what Alex necessarily feels like or is comfortable presenting; on the whole, they have never really cared about how others perceive them, despite the existence of gender role pressure. In relation to dating and in contrast with their experiences as a younger person, Alex finds that people mostly respond positively to the news that they are autistic and/or transgender. This may, however, be influenced by their tendency to interact largely with other transgender and/or autistic people.

FINAL THOUGHTS

Alex's experience of being autistic and transgender has been largely positive, though their experience with the larger neurotypical world is more mixed. On the one hand, they take a lot of enjoyment out of their natural state as gender non-binary and autistic. However, the reaction of the world around them to these aspects of their being, and efforts to change and shape them to be more socially acceptable, has caused them a great deal of anguish. To a lesser extent, autism-related symptomatology, like executive dysfunction and anxiety, have also been problematic, particularly with regard to the expectations of the neurotypical world. Alex's response has been to move away from conventional understandings of autism as a disorder and towards acceptance of it, and themselves, as neurodiverse, transgender, and part of a community. They have found acceptance in the disabled and queer communities and, when needed, strength and solidarity against discrimination and pressure from the wider world.

Alex has found support from unexpected avenues as well. Though they no longer attend the conservative synagogue in which they were raised, their rabbi has been very supportive of their gender identity. Alex also takes inspiration from traditionally Jewish understandings of gender. Though not always the case with others interviewed, their parents have also been very supportive of both their autism and non-binary identity.

Alex's more positive experience, in comparison to others, may be because, at 21, they are the youngest participant by three years and societal expectations of gendered behaviour and the possibilities for those with autism are relatively more advanced. They also come from a relatively privileged background and, while they don't make a great deal of personal income, family wealth and social location grants them access to autism supports and services not available to all. Additionally, as is often required to obtain autism services and funding, Alex has an official diagnosis of autism. Still, Alex recalls a great deal of frustration with not being informed of their diagnosis until they were older, which is not uncommon among those interviewed.

Also not uncommon, Alex first began to explore their gender identity through MMORPGs. In fact, transgender gaming is garnering increased attention, with explorations on the topic including the appropriation of canonically cisgender game characters by transgender communities (e.g. head canon)[31] and the use of MMORPGs to explore gender and build communities that bridge the online and offline worlds.[32] More unique, among those interviewed, is Alex's exploration of sign language as a tool for when they are having trouble communicating. This is not, however, unusual and there have been publications that investigated this topic.[33,34] Perhaps we didn't hear more about this because we failed to explicitly ask. Unfortunately, Alex was not able to convince those around them to learn sign language as well, though they have continued to learn it as a second language.

ENDNOTES

1   Schnurr, 1999
2   Daybreak Game Company, 2010
3   BioWare Austin, 2011
4   Camp Kennebec, n.d.
5   Xtra, 2017
6   Autistics For Autistics, n.d.
7   The Centre for Addiction and Mental Health is a Toronto mental health service and hospital
8   Ontario Ministry of Children, Community and Social Services, n.d.
9   Devita-Raeburn & Spectrum, 2016
10 Ringo, 2013
11 Dempsey, 2018
12 Monsebraaten, 2018
13 The word incel is a portmanteau of involuntarily celibate and an online community of predominantly white cis men who tend to externalize their self-identified inability "to get a romantic or sexual partner…[to] the cruelness of women" (Mezzofiore, 2018).
14 Fonrobert, n.d.
15 Kukla, 2006
16 Qalonymous ben Qalonymous ben Me'ir & Habermann, 1956
17 Cuil Press, n.d.
18 A traditional Jewish bathing ritual.
19 Kupferstein, 2018
20 Cassidy & Rodgers, 2017
21 Richa *et al.*, 2014
22 Adams, Hitomi, & Moody, 2017
23 Weiss & Fardella, 2018
24 Gordon, 2017
25 Cendrowski, 2007
26 Shore & DePaul, 2017
27 Ferguson & Saines, & Jackson, 2010
28 Sugar, 2013
29 Another word for non-autistic, or neurotypical.
30 Johnson & Levinson, 1988

31 Dym, Brubaker, & Fiesler, 2018
32 Baume, 2016
33 Autism Canada, 2017
34 Bonvillian, Nelson, & Rhyne, 1981

GRACE

Grace is a 35-year-old Caucasian transgender woman, born in Canada and currently living in Toronto, who identifies as queer and bisexual/pansexual. A federal public servant, she is self-diagnosed as autistic. Grace came out as a transgender woman about two years ago and, due to her employment, has opted to use a pseudonym. She uses she/her pronouns.

COMING OUT AS AUTISTIC

While never formally diagnosed with autism, Grace had suspected there was something different about her since she was about nine or ten years old, though she couldn't grasp what it might be. Her parents also noticed that there was something odd about her interpersonal interactions around this time and subsequently made an appointment with the school psychologist, which she resented and resisted as a way of being stigmatized, particularly in light of her existing diagnosis of obsessive-compulsive disorder (OCD). In high school, Grace started to hear and read more about autism and Asperger's and immediately recognized herself in the descriptions she saw. She didn't pursue a diagnosis though, as she was relatively content having a small but close group of friends, while "mystifying most of the other kids." Grace has, over time, become more certain that she is "somewhere on the spectrum," but is able to hide it by "feigning normality when necessary."

This has been a double-edged sword; while Grace attributes her success in school and work to hiding her autism, it has also resulted in a great deal of internalized ableism. For instance, when she recognizes similar thought processes and behaviours in others, she can become vicariously anxious and embarrassed. Grace often finds herself caught between identifying closely with the other person and trying to distance herself from them in order to avoid drawing potentially negative attention to herself. Overall, she has always tried to "keep [her] head down and stay in the background" in order to avoid being "put on the spot in any way, unless exquisitely prepared." Grace describes her experience of coming out as autistic as, initially, a "grudging acknowledgement of…this is one more way [she'll] never be normal." She has, however, become more self-accepting and confident in recent years, which she connects to a better understanding of her capabilities and how autism isn't inherently good or bad but does impact the way she functions in the world.

COMING OUT AS TRANSGENDER

Grace didn't recall there being a single moment when she knew she wasn't cisgender. Rather, she recalls a series of "brief flashes," beginning when she was four or five, of uncertainty around her gender in a manner that she retrospectively identifies as questioning. Certainty, as she states, "came much later."

Grace credits the television show *My Little Pony*[1] with helping her to realize that she is transgender. She first became involved in this fandom via the social media blogging site Tumblr around 2010, and gradually became more aware of transgender issues through the blogs of others who were also beginning to explore their gender identity. This is, in fact, a common phenomenon.[2,3] Grace notes that a common joke in that community, many years into the fandom's existence, is that bronies[4] "end up being super gay and trans, or else outright Nazis."

In any case, beginning in 2010, Grace started gradually to think about her gender identity. By 2014, though she was still fighting to suppress these feelings, she had moved from being certain about being cisgender to "not as certain about that as [she] used to be." It was around this period that Grace became friends with more transgender people and, as a result, invested in educating herself in order to counter the transphobic and transmisogynist attitudes she picked up from gay cisgender male culture.

Grace identifies "The Big Epiphany" about being transgender as taking place during the summer of 2017. She was, at that time, reading the science fiction novel *Dreadnought*,[5] which is about a closeted transgender girl who is initially unable to come out. This character inherits superhero powers which reshape her body to align with her internal understanding of her gender as female. Grace recalls that she had three reactions to this in close succession: "Man, she's so lucky, I wish that could happen to me"; "Holy shit, where did that come from?"; and "You know exactly where that came from." This moment opened the flood gates and allowed Grace to think more about her body image and identity. She speculated for some time about being non-binary, before coming to the conclusion that she was in fact a woman.

Grace subsequently came out to those closest to her, including her long-time best friend, partner, and friends from Tumblr, all of whom were supportive. Although she waffled a bit, she decided to pursue medical transition by late December 2017 and told the rest of her friendship group, many of whom she played *World of Warcraft*[6] with, by spring 2018. She had hesitated to do so because a couple in this group were right-wing Christians who had expressed negative sentiments about gay marriage and even explicitly told her that, as a queer person, she shouldn't have human rights. On that occasion, the other group members hadn't openly supported her, and she was concerned that if she came out, something similar would happen. Grace resolved this by coming out to everyone but these two in a smaller group chat in order to explain why she was uncomfortable in their presence. As it happened, her friends agreed with her and supported her by excluding them from the group.

In June 2018, Grace came out to her parents, in part because she needed them to understand why she was so alarmed by the prospect of a social conservative being elected the Premier of her province. She reports that, while they weren't negative, they were ignorant. Grace was able to convince them to read some materials[7] she sent and to attend a local PFLAG (Parents and Friends of Lesbians and Gays) group that they have since come to enjoy. Overall, she appreciates the effort that they are making, though they continue occasionally to have difficulty with pronouns.

In November 2018, after informing her boss and two former co-workers and receiving a legal name change, Grace came out officially at work. While her co-workers have been fairly supportive, her boss has been incredibly, almost surprisingly, helpful. Before coming out, she joined an employee lesbian, gay, bisexual, transgender, queer (or sometimes questioning), and two-spirited (LGBTQ2+) advisory group at the human resources department of the federal government agency she works for. As a member of this group, she was able to advocate that a higher priority be given to policies relating to transgender employees. When nothing had been done by early 2018, Grace chaired a committee working group on this issue. She wrote much of this policy, which was subsequently adopted by the advisory group and has become a draft for others to draw on. When she came out to her boss, she was able to reference this policy which was, at the time, being sent to senior management for approval. Grace relays that her boss, "without being prompted and without having dealt with a trans employee ever before," unknowingly followed her policy exactly.

LINKS BETWEEN AUTISM AND GENDER IDENTITY

Though she isn't sure of the cause and effect, Grace observes that most of the transgender people she knows identify as being on the autism spectrum. She notes, however, that this may be the result of choosing to interact with people with whom she is naturally more comfortable. Grace also wonders whether autism affected her ability to explore her gender identity; for instance, did her difficulties with relating to other people interfere with thinking about her gender identity? Or, alternatively, does she have difficulty understanding or empathizing with others because she didn't fully understand herself until recently?

FAMILY

Grace is an only child and has a good relationship with her parents and grandfather, who lives with them. She does not, however, have any contact with her extended family, who she finds small-minded and ignorant. Her parents have been largely supportive of her female identity, though they continue to have trouble with things like pronouns. Nevertheless, her mother has been very happy to reconnect with her as a woman, including shopping for clothing with her, and, recently, telling her that she'd always wanted a daughter. Grace is not aware of any other out transgender people in her family and feels sure that her parents would have mentioned this if it was the case. She does, however, have a vague sense that some extended and long-deceased family members might have been autistic.

COMMUNITY AND ACTIVISM

Grace is not very involved in the autism or transgender communities, largely because she sees herself as a homebody who is not brave enough for activism. She does follow the issues that are important in the broader community and tends to participate vicariously through her partner, who is involved in the transgender and autistic community both professionally and as an activist. She wouldn't, for instance, have attended the Philadelphia Transgender Wellness Conference[8] for two years in a row were it not for accompanying her partner. Likewise, she has met a number of other transgender activists through her partner.

WORK

As noted, Grace works for the Federal Government of Canada in a professional capacity. Despite this being an "enforcement-minded" agency with gendered social conventions, she has found her workplace, and, in particular, her boss, to be incredibly supportive of her transition. Nevertheless, Grace's workplace experience is relatively unusual among those interviewed, and the greater economic power afforded by her professional role may be a factor in this.

While Grace's current workplace is a good fit with regards to her autism, this has not always been the case. Her profession, for instance, requires a post-degree internship. Unfortunately, between gendered and neurotypical social expectations and conventions, she had a great deal of trouble obtaining one and was frequently told she was, euphemistically, not "the right fit." Grace attributes this, in part, to not being able to feign small talk with potential employers, "appreciate fancy suits, or talk sports." As a result, she was forced to accept an internship with an unscrupulous employer who exploited and underpaid her.

HEALTHCARE

In addition to autism and gender identity disorder, Grace has received diagnoses of OCD, social anxiety, and clinical depression. Like most others interviewed, her healthcare experiences have been mixed. She recalls, for instance, that even the prospect of an autism diagnosis made her feel potentially stigmatized when she was younger, a fear that her school's psychologist did little to assuage. She resisted treatment for OCD for similar reasons, though it had begun to seriously affect her quality of life by high school.

Grace didn't pursue mental healthcare of her own volition until the last year of her degree, when she visited her university's healthcare service because she was depressed and had been suicidal for a long time. She was seen by a GP who immediately put her on a high dose of Escitalopram and referred her to further mental healthcare services. Grace attended two appointments through this service before receiving a further referral to a psychiatrist who practiced Freudian psychoanalysis.

Grace saw him for psychoanalytically oriented therapy four times a week for four years, largely because he was covered by her public health insurance, and it gave her an excuse to miss work at a job she hated. However, he "irritated [Grace] for a number of reasons." He tended, for instance, to fall asleep while she was talking to him, which she suspects was due to narcolepsy and his advanced age. He also lacked a basic understanding of modern technology, including the internet, where much of her social life was based, and dismissed her online friends as not truly real. On the whole, Grace found that, while he would have been considered very progressive in the past, his understanding of gender and sexuality halted around 1990. For example, "his standing theory was that [she] wanted to be straight, no matter what [she] said" and, as a result, she never felt comfortable bringing up her concerns around gender with him.

Grace also continued to see this psychiatrist because he helped her to find a psychiatric medication regimen that worked for her and continued to prescribe it without question, which many others were hesitant to do. For instance, when she briefly moved from Ontario to British Columbia, which she described as having a "crisis-level shortage of family doctors," she was forced to accept a GP listed as available through the provincial College of Physicians and Surgeons. This GP complained about and refused to prescribe half of the medication she was on. She continued, as a result, to rely on the aforementioned psychiatrist for prescriptions until returning to Ontario, when she found a GP who would continue to prescribe her medication regimen.

Overall, Grace has not been thrilled by the quality of mental healthcare she has received. She would, for instance, have preferred to have pursued therapy that wasn't (as she termed it) "Freudian bullshit." Coverage for the services of therapists and psychologists, however, is severely limited by both provincial healthcare and her federal employee health insurance, which left her with few options. Grace has, as a result, resigned herself to accepting as good enough the quality of healthcare that is available to her and, in general, feels "more or less stable most of the time." In any case, she reports that her mood has significantly improved since meeting her partner and starting the process of transition.

Grace is currently receiving transitional healthcare from her GP, who initially wanted to refer her to Toronto's Sherbourne Health Centre,[9] which is known for providing transgender-specific healthcare. Grace didn't want to accept this referral because she was aware that this clinic has a very long waiting list. Instead, she chose to educate her GP about providing transgender healthcare, starting by introducing her to the provincially accepted guidelines for this area of practice.[10] Grace describes this experience as a "mixed bag," as her GP has been rigid in following the proffered guidelines. As a result, while she has agreed to provide hormone replacement therapy (estrogen), she has also been very reluctant to deviate from the recommended dosages and protocols, even when Grace's individual circumstances recommend it. She has had a similar experience with the psychologist she is seeing for a surgery recommendation letter. Though Grace is generally happy with her, she is also frustrated by the psychologist's insistence on strictly adhering to the Standards of Care[11] for fear of sanction from her professional college or provincial healthcare provider.

Grace relayed another incident where she had an issue with her genitals which she had thought might be related to hormone replacement therapy. Her GP initially considered referring her to a men's clinic and, when Grace visibly grimaced at this suggestion, recalled a new urologist heading the local transgender surgery program. Grace subsequently saw this specialist a few times and, while he was pleasant and informative about the forthcoming transgender surgery program, she found him unhelpful and only superficially concerned with her particular medical concern. She's since heard similar concerns from other transgender people. Otherwise, Grace is generally satisfied with her healthcare, though she was frustrated by her dentist, who for some time misgendered her and demanded to know what her medication was for.

MEDIA REPRESENTATION

Grace hasn't seen much representation of transgender or autistic people in the mainstream media beyond "horrific, simplified, and/or sensationalist exaggerations" that don't reflect her own experience. As a result, she tends to seek out "good queer content" in non-mainstream media like fanworks, indie comics, and podcasts, which she has found to have more realistic depictions of queer relationships. Grace is particularly drawn to romance, and it is in this genre of fanfiction and fanart that she first saw herself represented. She has since created fanart herself to work out and explore different feelings.

SOCIAL RULES

Long before exploring her gender identity, Grace realized that she had no interest in the stereotypical trappings of masculinity, like sports, cars, and "bro culture." Rather, as a member of her school's gifted program from grade two through graduation, she and her friends were "nerds" and largely outside the "normative expectations" regarding, for instance, dating. More broadly, Grace relates that she is often treated as "weird" in an undefinable way, though she doubts others suspect her specifically of being autistic. She believes that it is probably difficult for others to tell because she has become so accustomed to performing neurotypical behaviour in public and doesn't openly identify as autistic to anyone but her friends and other autistic people.

Grace does relate having difficulty making new friendships to her autism. For instance, she often relies heavily on shared interests or participation in events (such as board game nights at a local pub) to acclimatize herself to new people. Even then, she only feels capable of joining a new social group by "low-key insinuating [herself] into it" over a long period of time. For Grace, this means arriving early to events in order to interact with other attendees prior to a crowd or in-groups forming, which she finds intimidating.

Grace compares her experiences in making active efforts at socialization to playing the computer game *The Sims*,[12] which allows players to create human-like characters (Sims) in a virtual "dollhouse," and watch them engage in relationships, jobs, and hobbies. Sims's need for social contact is expressed in an onscreen meter that tracks their mood. The player can direct individual Sims to take specific actions in order to refill this meter and therefore improve and maintain a positive mood. While these actions sometimes backfire and deplete the meter, the player can determine which actions always achieve a positive result through trial and error. In contrast with *The Sims*, Grace feels that real-world social rules and expectations are a lot less predictable and more arbitrary, and she is often uncertain about the results of her actions in social settings.

FINAL THOUGHTS

Grace is a 35-year-old Caucasian transgender woman who lives in Toronto. Resourceful and intelligent, she has a close circle of friends and family who love and support her. Though she doesn't consider herself "brave enough" to be an activist, she nonetheless advocates for herself and others through the creation of policies and provision of educational resources. Grace has experienced some success in using games and gaming of various types as both a medium of communication and a metaphor for navigating a world with seemingly arbitrary, invisible rules.

Though both Grace and her family suspected she was neurodevelopmentally "atypical" as a child, she has resisted diagnosis or treatment for fear of being further stigmatized. She revisited this in high school, and while she ultimately hasn't pursued a formal diagnosis, she has accepted herself as a member of the autistic community. However, she still struggles with internalized ableism.

Grace was similarly reluctant to accept mental healthcare until forced, due to OCD, long-standing depression, and suicidality, near the end of her university education. While she has ultimately found a medication regime that works for her, she had to navigate an unsympathetic and, at times, hostile healthcare landscape in the process. Grace has had particular difficulties finding a GP who will continue to prescribe her medication and, as a result of this and restrictions on health insurance coverage, has had to rely on a narcoleptic and homophobic psychoanalyst for many years.

Grace's pathway to accepting herself as a woman had a similar trajectory. There was no single moment when she "knew" she was transgender. Instead, Grace had complicated feelings about gender from a very young age and, though she tried to suppress them, ultimately came to terms with her gender identity. She partially credits the *My Little Pony* fandom, which has a large transfeminine component, as crucial in prompting her to explore her gender more closely. Through it she learned of several blogs by other transfeminine people who shared similar narratives. Grace also consumes a large amount of non-mainstream queer and transgender media and even participates in making some.

Grace ultimately came out as transgender in stages; first to her partner and close friends, then to her larger friendship group, parents, and work. Despite some hiccups along the way, she has been largely supported, especially by her mother and boss. Grace has, in fact, written a policy for transgender employees that she has been able to rely on through this process. In this sense, she was able to, quite literally, dictate how her workplace managed and supported her. This is in contrast with her profession more generally, which has not always been accommodating of her disabilities, and isn't known for having a nuanced understanding of gendered social norms. Grace feels more mixed about her experiences with transgender healthcare as, while she has been able to have many of her needs met through persistent self-advocacy, she is often frustrated by nonsensical gatekeeping and overreliance on medical guidelines. She is, however, generally satisfied so far.

ENDNOTES

1 Thiessen *et al.*, 2010
2 Sidney, n.d.
3 Faraday, 2014
4 Male-identified fans of *My Little Pony*.
5 Daniel, 2017
6 Blizzard Entertainment, 2004
7 Brill, 2016
8 Philadelphia Transgender Wellness Conference, n.d.
9 Sherbourne Health Centre, n.d.
10 Bourns, 2016
11 Coleman *et al.*, 2012
12 Maxis, 2000

ISABELLA

Isabella is a 29-year-old transgender woman, who identifies as asexual and homoromantic.[1] She was born and currently lives in Toronto, and is of Chinese and Vietnamese descent. She was diagnosed as autistic when she was quite young and has been out as transgender for a number of years. Isabella opted to be identifiable in this interview. She uses she/her pronouns.

COMING OUT AS AUTISTIC

Isabella was formally diagnosed with Asperger's syndrome by her school therapist when she was four years old. It was, at this time, considered to be a less severe form of autism[2] and she was offended when it was merged with autism, as she considers herself to be a person with a "mental variation," rather than like these "more extreme cases." Isabella was also diagnosed with ADHD (predominantly inattentive) and dyslexia, the latter of which makes reading difficult, particularly Chinese characters.

Isabella dismisses the possibility that ADHD and Asperger's are directly related and is similarly frustrated by the degree to which her gender dysphoria is falsely attributed to Asperger's. She does, however, see both ADHD and Asperger's as neurodiversities and aspects of herself that she, due to stigma, has had difficulty coming to terms with. Nevertheless, Isabella is somewhat skeptical of the different labels given to her and their basis in, or relevance to, her lived experience.

While her parents have always known she has Asperger's, and her cousins and siblings have been largely supportive, Isabella has had a difficult time "coming out" to her aunts and uncles. She worried that, while these relatives knew she was "different," they wouldn't understand what Asperger's was and would see it as "adding shame to the family." As a result, Isabella felt immense pressure to hide her Asperger's by trying not to talk too much, or about things she was passionate about, which was largely unsuccessful. On one occasion, for example, she was watching sports with her relatives and, while they focused on who was winning, she couldn't stop fixating on and talking about the players' uniforms.

After some of Isabella's younger cousins and older relatives on her mother's side were diagnosed with autism, however, their parents became more understanding and sympathetic. One aunt in particular has one son with autism and another with a physical disability, and is considered to be a "second mom to everyone." Still, Isabella finds it frustrating when people treat her differently after becoming aware of her Asperger's, particularly because, though the judgment is often mild, it is expressed through non-verbal behaviour.

COMING OUT AS TRANSGENDER

While Isabella identifies as a transgender female, she has also been called "bianxing"[3] (變性) by other Taiwanese-Canadian and Chinese-Canadian queer youths. She has also been called two-spirited[4] by some Ojibwe friends. The path to self-acceptance has been long, starting when she first realized, at four years old, that something about her was "odd...[and] not right." Isabella was aware, at the time, that she related more to girls than boys and was confused about how they differed physically. "The first symptom of being a trans girl" occurred when she was four-and-a-half and showered with her female-bodied cousin. Isabella recalls seeing her cousin's vulva and thinking that, as she grew older, her "package would shrink and fall off" to reveal one.

Isabella's next memory is of puberty and "overcompensating for [the female identity] she was afraid of." She recalls, for instance, hearing the term "trans" in grade eight and, realizing both that she identified with it on some level and that it might be used to target her, she "became a bully" pre-emptively. Between 12 and 18 years old she was "a total jerk ass…[who] indulged in toxic masculinity" and is grateful that she wasn't aware of incels[5] or other similarly toxic groups. Fortunately, over time, she realized that this attitude was a product of her own insecurity.

After starting college, Isabella began to identify as a "feminine man" and realized that she was, in some way, "trans." After this revelation she slowly became more aware of gender dysphoria and, in 2013, realized that she had to try and explore, rather than continue to "shove away," her femininity. Isabella characterized the following year as "kind of amazing" in that she was, for the first time, able to feel freer in her self-expression and explore a part "of the world that she had been blinded to." Overall, she is glad that she has had the opportunity to explore who she is and is now in the process of slowly transitioning.

However, in losing male privilege, Isabella began to experience sexual harassment, like being catcalled and solicited publicly. She also experiences a great deal of anxiety around the potential for violent transphobia, and is aware that anything can happen "the moment she walks out her door" if people so much as suspect she is transgender. It is difficult, as a result, for her to go "outside her safe bubble."

Isabella worried that she "would lose most of her friends and be shunned by her family" if she came out as transgender. As a result, she tested the water by coming out to those she felt would be the most accepting first. For instance, Isabella told her brothers and, when they responded positively, informed her cousins by Facebook messenger. She then told her younger aunts and uncles and, while some had trouble accepting it, all were ultimately supportive. However, Isabella has not yet told her parents or all of her older relatives. Her difficulties in this regard include the emotional labour involved, and linguistic barriers that make it difficult to accurately describe the concepts of gender dysphoria and non-conformity. Isabella did attempt to come out to her parents, which they unfortunately took poorly. Her mother didn't say anything, finished cleaning the dishes before walking out of the room, and has since pretended that the conversation didn't happen. Her father, however, responded by ignorantly conflating being queer to mental illness, which made her very angry.

LINKS BETWEEN AUTISM AND GENDER IDENTITY

Isabella strongly disagreed when asked whether autism and gender identity are linked and expressed frustration that people conflate the two. She notes, for instance, that she has cousins who are cisgender and autistic, and knows others who are transgender and not autistic. Isabella opines that they may appear to be connected because a lot of autistic people are more open to exploring gendered aspects of themselves than neurotypical people constrained by social rules and expectations. She likens this to the "false parallel" between borderline personality disorder and gender dysphoria,[6] which she attributes to misunderstanding and mental health stigma. Isabella also points out that queer youth have a heightened awareness of and exposure to mental health issues, compared to their cisgender and straight counterparts, due to stigma and trauma. In the absence of this trauma and "bullshit…we wouldn't need all these safe spaces, [or] have so much depression."

FAMILY

As noted, Isabella's family have been very supportive of her as a person with Asperger's, particularly after several other family members received similar diagnoses. But while her extended family and brothers have been supportive of her identity as female, it is still an area of conflict for her parents. In fact, Isabella's mother refuses to address the issue, while her father has rejected it as a deviance.

COMMUNITY AND ACTIVISM

Isabella used to participate in a transgender youth group[7] and drop-in,[8] and volunteer with a program[9] that provides counselling, homelessness, and suicide crisis services to LGBT youth. Though she has never participated in any solely autistic communities, she did meet several autistic people in these groups. Currently, however, she is working longer hours in order to save towards an apartment and is now busy when these groups meet. Still, she is involved in online communities and continues to chat with friends from several Toronto area queer spaces. Isabella is also worried that she will have a difficult time in the dating world if others know she is neurodivergent, particularly in light of the issues she already experiences as an asexual, homoromantic, transgender woman. Indeed, she often finds that "the only people who want to date [her] are cis straight guys."

WORK

As noted, Isabella works quite a bit—on average, eight to ten-hour shifts. She recently began working more in order to save money towards her own apartment, which she hopes will launch her towards future job goals. While she is currently quite successful in this arena, Isabella worries that she may have trouble finding work if employers know she is Asperger's.

HEALTHCARE

Isabella openly identifies as "non-op," meaning that she is "not interested in ever getting bottom surgery." On the whole, Isabella characterizes her healthcare experience, as a person who is both transgender and autistic, as "not a big deal." She does, however, find that hospitals are challenging because, when there, she frequently has to correct people on her name and pronouns. Prior to beginning hormone replacement therapy, Isabella took the opportunity to bank her sperm with a local fertility clinic as she plans to become a mother in the future. She was particularly glad that she didn't have to rely on the Centre for Addiction and Mental Health's (CAMH) gender clinic to begin hormone replace therapy and was instead able to attain this through her regular doctor and endocrinologist, both of whom she describes as "very supportive and easy going."

With the exception of the ten-year period (1998–2008) in which transgender surgery was delisted from the public insurer,[10] and between 2016 and the present day,[11] the Clarke Institute of Psychiatry, and later CAMH, was "the only way to access [publicly insured] transition-related healthcare."[12] Though it has improved significantly since the public insurer[13] relisted services, particularly since they ceased to be the sole point of access in 2016, its historical reputation is abysmal. It was, in particular, notorious for its traumatizing, sexist, and overly rigid approach and characterized by exceptionally low rates of approval for transitional healthcare (less than 10% by some accounts).[14,15]

Isabella attended a special education class from kindergarten to grade seven. She described the program as providing a substandard education that caused her to fall behind, especially in science and English. For this reason, and while she appreciated the opportunity to interact with other students with learning disabilities, she opted for the academic stream in grade eight. Aside from an academic accommodation assessment in college, she hasn't received support for Asperger's since high school.

MEDIA REPRESENTATION

Isabella almost never sees media representation of people who, like herself, are "homoromantic, asexual, and moderately conservative." What she does see are straight and "white-passing" transgender people who share the typical narrative of "a boy trapped in a girl's body." In contrast to popular media, which also shows hardly any people of colour and focuses on celebrities, the transgender community contains a "huge constellation" of individuals and experiences. Non-binary people and intersex people are, for example, left almost entirely out of the conversation and, when represented, their experiences are conflated with those of transgender people.

SOCIAL RULES

Isabella's experience with social rules varies according to the environment she's in. She is, for example, more likely to be open about her identity when she feels safe, as she does with store employees in downtown Toronto, and her friends who see her as two-spirit on the reserve where she goes fishing. In these circumstances, Isabella will confidently correct people on her gender identity and pronouns. She doesn't correct people in rural areas, which she sees as "white dominated," because she worries men will assault her for being too effeminate.

FINAL THOUGHTS

Isabella is a 29-year-old, transgender, asexual, and homo-romantic woman of Chinese and Vietnamese heritage. Born and currently living in Toronto, she was diagnosed with Asperger's when she was four years old, prior to its inclusion within the larger autism spectrum. As a result, Isabella sees her experience with Asperger's as different from, and less severe than, those with autism. She has also considered the relationship between autism and gender identity and concluded that, though unrelated in origin, they do interact in manifestation. Autistic people may, for instance, be more inclined to question their gender identity due to being less constrained by social rules and limitations.

Isabella first suspected that she was transgender when she was about four years old, though she lacked the words for it. She broached the issue, over the ensuing years, slowly and cautiously, always aware of the stigma attached to this kind of difference. Indeed, there was a long period of time during Isabella's teens in which she described her reactionary behaviour against this aspect of herself as "toxic" and "bullying." Fortunately, after entering college, she was able to explore her gender identity more fully, embrace herself as a woman, and come out, in stages, to her friends and family. In the process, Isabella has tried on and had applied to her a variety of culturally specific gender identity labels, like bianxing and two-spirit.

Isabella has since been involved in several groups and organizations for LGBT people. However, because of work commitments, she no longer has time to attend them. As a result, though she still keeps in touch with friends from these groups, Isabella now largely participates in discussions with transgender communities online. She is, on the whole, satisfied with her social life, though she worries about dating as a neurodiverse, asexual, homoromantic, transgender woman.

Despite the many positives of coming out as transgender, Isabella talked a lot about dealing with transphobic violence and misogyny, particularly on the street. This is a relatively recent experience for her and has a big impact on her decisions to stay close to home, where she feels safer, rather than venture into less urban environments. And while Isabella has a supportive primary medical team, she also experiences transphobic discrimination when forced to deal with unfamiliar healthcare providers, as at hospitals. She is particularly glad that her experience of transgender healthcare never involved gender clinics.

Isabella's family is large, multi-generational, and close knit. In addition to her parents and brothers, she has several aunts, uncles, and cousins, most of whom she sees or interacts with, at least online, regularly. Their support and acceptance of Isabella, with regards to Asperger's and as a transgender woman, has been mixed. On the one hand, while difficult for older family members to understand initially, they are supportive of her Asperger's, especially since several of her cousins received similar diagnoses. Isabella's brothers and extended family had a similar reaction to her gender identity, despite some concerns about linguistic barriers, and ultimately came to accept it. On the other hand, her parents have been unable to incorporate this information into their lives and, as yet, are unwilling to accept her gender identity.

Isabella's description of special education was especially astute. In her eight-year tenure in this program, she benefitted from meeting other students like herself, but received a substandard education. Fortunately, she had the option to choose a regular academic stream in grade eight. In fact, much has been written about the tendency of special education classrooms to isolate learners rather than prepare them for academic achievement.[16,17]

ENDNOTES

1   Homoromantic defines people who are romantically, though not necessarily sexually, attracted to people of the same gender as themselves, while asexual delineates a person who does not experience sexual attraction (Paramo, 2016).

2   Barahona-Correa & Filipe, 2015
3   A Mandarin word, bianxing translates literally to "changed heart" and figuratively to "change sex" (Koetse, 2015).
4   "Two-spirit refers to a person who identifies as having both a masculine and a feminine spirit, and is used by some indigenous people to describe their sexual, gender and/or spiritual identity" (Re:searching for LGBTQ2S+ Health, n.d.).
5   See definition in note 13 for "Alex" above.
6   Thom, 2016
7   Supporting Our Youth, n.d.
8   The 519, n.d.
9   Egale Canadian Human Rights Trust, n.d.
10 Graffeo, Brown, & Freeman, 2019
11 Centre for Addiction and Mental Health, n.d.
12 Hitomi, 2018, p.81
13 Ontario Health Insurance Plan
14 Rowe, 2009
15 Withers, n.d.
16 Aviv, 2018
17 Butrymowicz, 2017

JAMES

James is a 36-year-old Caucasian transgender man from England, who identifies as gay, and currently lives in London. He first suspected that he was autistic about eight years ago, after reading literature on the subject, and shortly before starting to question his gender identity. James is now awaiting an official assessment for autism. James is a pseudonym and his pronouns are he/him.

COMING OUT AS AUTISTIC

James first suspected that he was autistic when he was 28 years old, shortly before he began questioning his gender identity. He subsequently read a book that posits that autism is linked with "male" traits like systematizing, rather than those assigned female, like "empathizing," and that autistics have "extreme male brains."[1] James identified deeply with this concept, as it helped him to place his struggles with relationship empathy in context and understand that there wasn't anything inherently wrong with him. Dr. Baron-Cohen's book[2] also prompted him to explore his gender identity and, at first, whether his autistic traits might be due to being transgender. For instance, James initially questioned whether his desire to be male was because men are supposed to be less socially competent, though he ultimately came to realize that he was both autistic and transgender.

James scored very high on the online Autism Quotient test,[3] developed by Dr. Baron-Cohen,[4] and is continuing to read about autistic traits and behaviours in order to better understand himself. He has, however, had difficulty "coming out" as autistic, especially to his family and those closest to him. When he does disclose his autism, he has found that the term itself provides a helpful shorthand for others to understand his behaviour and mannerisms.

James has struggled for a long time to get an autism diagnosis through the National Health Service (NHS). He wonders if being assigned female is interfering with this process and notes that female children in particular are pushed to develop strategies to mask autistic traits, in order to perform expected feminine behaviours.[5] It may, as a result, be difficult for family to accept that their children are autistic as adults when they have camouflaged their autism so well and for so long. With regard to seeking a diagnosis, James has found that diagnosticians and other medical professionals often take his ability to make eye contact as evidence that he cannot be autistic. His family has also made similar statements, and he hasn't felt comfortable speaking to them about autism again. James is hopeful that a diagnosis will help him to broach this topic with his family again.

COMING OUT AS TRANSGENDER

Although James had suspected that he was transgender for some time, it wasn't until watching the documentary *The Boy Who Was Born a Girl*[6] that things really "clicked." The story immediately resonated with him, though he still needed to think about and process the idea for a number of years. It was in this period that James struggled with shame, internalized transphobia, and concern for family and friends' reactions.

James decided that he needed to transition after ending a long-term relationship in 2013. He had identified as a butch lesbian during this period, because he assumed that his masculine traits meant he must be and had also suspected that his strongly lesbian-identified partner wouldn't have accepted him coming out as or transitioning to male. In retrospect, James wonders whether shame prevented him from giving her the benefit of the doubt. He began to see a therapist following the break-up, which gave him the chance to explore his gender identity in a safe environment and led to his decision to do what "feels right." In the process of transitioning to male, James made a whole new group of friends in the transgender community and at groups like FTM London[7] and TransBareAll.[8] He also, unexpectedly, reconnected with a childhood friend who was coming out as a transgender woman. James characterizes the process of transitioning, though very stressful, as the best thing he ever did for himself.

James describes the period of his life in which he identified as a lesbian as "almost asexual." He continued to identify as asexual for a long time after starting transition, before coming to realize that he is "90 percent gay." While he wonders if this is due to something intrinsic that would lead him to be homosexual in any gender, he partially ascribes it to a heightened sex drive after beginning testosterone,[9] in which he found himself watching largely gay porn, despite never having viewed porn at all before. His understanding of himself as a gay man developed further during a long-term relationship with a non-binary person. There is, in fact, a growing body of research supporting change in sexual identity around transition.[10,11] One study found that 64 percent of those who transitioned reported a change in sexual attractions post transition.[12]

LINKS BETWEEN AUTISM AND GENDER IDENTITY

James is aware of research showing a link between gender identity and autism and wonders if transgender and autistic people may be more likely to use hormones and other medical interventions to bring their gender presentation and identity into alignment. For instance, he had a hard time when his therapist encouraged him to explore and be comfortable with uncertainty around gender identity and presentation, as it ran counter to his own need to categorize and see things in black and white. When James first started transitioning he wanted to be as like a cisgender man as possible and, for a long time, to have lower surgery. He found, however, that the rigid thinking that characterized his autism led him to need a "perfect" result, which he did not feel was possible. James also expressed concern with the idea of giving over control of his body to a surgeon. Over time, he has come to embrace his identity as both transgender and male, and no longer wants lower surgery.

FAMILY

Though James had worried that his family would react negatively when he came out as transgender, they were almost unanimously supportive. The only person who reacted poorly was an extended family member, who wrote an email to him accusing him of lying to them. James attributed this to their personality, which differs from the rest of his family's more laid-back and liberal attitudes. He hasn't come out to them as gay yet, largely because, after coming out to them so many other times, he feels it's redundant.

In light of their acceptance of his gender identity, James finds his family's dismissiveness towards his autism strange, particularly since many are mental health professionals. Nevertheless, he was met with dismissal and told not to be silly when he talked to them about this. Others have opined that James "doesn't seem to be autistic" and that it is, in any case, a negative trait. He finds this both invalidating and reflective of the taboos and stereotypes surrounding autism.

COMMUNITY AND ACTIVISM

James is involved in several online and in-person groups for transgender, autistic, and kinky people and, as a result, most of his friends are transgender, or otherwise involved in these communities. They are a source of support and solidarity, helping him to navigate common problems, rather than continuing to do so on his own. Groups associated with the autistic community, in particular, have helped him to identify repetitive behaviours and patterns and whether they are changeable, or inherent due to autism.

WORK

James worked as a research assistant for a veterinary college on a project involving close collaboration with Chinese researchers. His job required frequent travel to China and networking with these researchers and their institutions. James initially worried that coming out as transgender, in order to transition, would put the project and his job in jeopardy. However, he was unexpectedly contacted by a stealth[13] transgender man at work, who, having seen him at transgender community events, was able to provide support and advice to him in this situation. This man put James in touch with a counsellor, who helped him process the situation, and ultimately to arrange a meeting with his employer. Despite his fears, his employer was immediately supportive of his need to transition in the workplace, accommodating him by reassigning him to another project within the same working group and sending an email to all employees affirming his support.

James's experiences of employment as an autistic person have been more mixed. Overall, a scientific career has been a good fit, because it utilizes his autistic traits and he is able to work with others who also appreciate a structured environment.

Even in this environment, however, James still struggles to understand social expectations and cues. For instance, he often needs to read work emails several times in order to unearth nuances and construct a neurotypical reply. James finds this process exhausting and anxiety-inducing, but also necessary in order to avoid issues with co-workers, as in the past he has been accused of being "terse." He has found that adding seemingly purposeless and "flowery" language to work communication helps to avoid this. Perhaps surprisingly, James's work has been far more accommodating of his gender identity than his autism.

HEALTHCARE

James's counsellor is very supportive and has helped him both at work and, more generally, to feel comfortable as a transgender man. However, he has been met with a great deal of gatekeeping when attempting to access transitional services, such as when his GP refused to refer him to a gender clinic which, in the UK, is necessary to receive transitional care. Though James received this referral after writing a letter of complaint to the practice manager, his GP refused to continue to prescribe or administer the testosterone authorized by the gender clinic, arguing that he had no experience and was concerned that James might regret it. James again complained to the practice manager, leading to a meeting between all five GPs, wherein they decided they were not prepared to follow through prescribing or administering the medication. James was then forced to find another GP, who has also resisted refilling prescriptions and forced James to shoulder the burden of tracking the need for blood work to monitor his hormone levels. He attributed this to, among other issues, a lack of experience with transgender people that is common across the medical professions.[14]

James's one positive experience with a GP, as regards transitional healthcare, was with a doctor who was a gay man and very senior in his practice. This GP was very supportive, despite James being his first transgender patient, and amenable to prescribing the contraception pill to stop his periods, while acknowledging that it wasn't a typical use and might have side effects. This was the first time he had felt that a doctor respected his agency.

James's experience of autism healthcare has also been quite challenging. Despite letters of support from his therapist, both his GP and psychologists have refused either to refer him for an autism assessment or to conduct the assessment because, for instance, he "makes too much eye contact" and their belief that, even if he were autistic, he would be on the mild end and not need a diagnosis. James disagrees, arguing that it is stressful and frustrating to be constantly told his experience is not what he says it is, and that a diagnosis would affirm his conception of himself and the world around him, while giving him access to needed supports. He suspects this gatekeeping may be partially because these practitioners are hesitant to "burden" the country's public health service.[15] In spite of medical gatekeeping, however, James finds autism has been a largely positive force in his life, particularly in the realms of healthcare navigation and self-advocacy. As a diligent, organized, and detail-oriented person, he is able to self-advocate more effectively by making lists, researching diagnoses, and preparing for medical appointments ahead of time.

James also has chronic fatigue syndrome and fibromyalgia. He traces the onset of both to the stress he was under leading up to top surgery, from which he never fully recovered. He relates that this spiralled into a debilitating illness in 2017, and that he has been on medical leave from work since. Unfortunately, this has isolated him from his friendships at work and has impacted the coping strategies he uses to manage his autism, like working out with friends and running when stressed.

MEDIA REPRESENTATION

Although James has seen some representations of transgender people in the media, with the exception of *The Boy Who Was Born a Girl*, he hasn't seen much reflecting his experience as a transgender man. He is aware of a recent Channel 4 documentary,[16] but hasn't watched it and understands that it doesn't have a large representation of transmasculine people. James also noted that the BBC series *Boy Meets Girl*[17] had some positive and groundbreaking characterizations of transgender people.

Regarding autistic people, James has only ever seen media that portrays them as severely disabled and no media about those who are transgender as well, though he draws a connection between how they are both portrayed as tragic or comic figures. He is aware of a number of programs with more "capable" characters like Sheldon, from *The Big Bang Theory*,[18] who are autistic coded without being explicitly named as such. James notes that, despite being more visible, the autistic traits of these characters tend to be used for comic relief, while autistic people in everyday situations are never seen.

SOCIAL RULES

James has had a lot of difficulty in identifying and differentiating between the social rules that used to apply to him as someone assigned female and someone now perceived to be cismale. For instance, he notes that there are many unspoken rules regarding how men interact when they're together and even in mixed groups. James has also had difficulty dating women and found himself wondering, for instance, if he should open the door for his date or put his arm around them. He recalls disliking this when he was seen as female but is unsure what other women might want. Similarly, though he has always done so, James now makes a point of noting and stopping himself from sitting with his legs widely spread, as men are seen as rude and taking up too much space for doing so. Ironically, he has had more trouble with these issues post transition, as before he saw himself as "just one of the guys," though he was also teased quite a bit in school for "acting mannish." Perhaps this speaks to the tension between being seen as masculine but not male and being seen as male but not masculine.

James recalls, in general, "never being very good at being female" and also wonders whether his dislike for "girly" clothes had something to do with an autistic preference for more comfortable clothing. He finds that he sometimes walks into dangerous situations because of his lack of perception. For instance, there have been quite a few instances where he has been alerted by his partner that strangers are hurling homophobic abuse at them. James relates this to his general obliviousness and wonders if this is related to his autism, to his tendency to see the best in people, or both.

FINAL THOUGHTS

James's journey to accepting and celebrating his autism and identity as a transgender man is a long and, ultimately, fulfilling one. Currently located in London, England, he is, at 36, the oldest of our, admittedly young, sample. James began actively exploring the possibility of being autistic, then transgender, in his late twenties, which he was prompted to do after reading a book on autism by Dr. Simon Baron-Cohen. Many autistic and transgender people find Baron-Cohen's extreme male brain and systematizing theories of autism problematic and even offensive. James, however, found them revelatory in accurately describing parts of his own experiences and helping him to better understand himself.

James assumed, before coming out as and transitioning to male, that his masculine traits meant that he was a butch lesbian, and though he did have a number of lesbian relationships, he never felt comfortable with his sexuality until after transitioning and coming out as "90 percent gay." Despite this, he has some regret for ending the relationship he was in just prior to transition. James did so because he assumed that his strongly lesbian-identified partner wouldn't be supportive. He now wonders whether this decision was influenced by his own internalized transphobia and shame.

James's immediate family and workplace, unlike many of those in the other interviews, have been quite supportive and accommodating of his transition. He has also made a number of connections within the local transgender community and with other transgender men since coming out as transgender. Unfortunately, James's experience of transitional healthcare, like many of those interviewed, has been somewhat lacking. He has, for instance, had difficulty finding a GP who will provide the necessary referrals and prescribe transitional care, for fear of his "regretting it," or due to the GP's professed lack of experience. James's one positive experience, in this regard, was with a GP who was senior in his practice and gay.

James's family were less supportive when he told them he suspected that he was autistic, and even his brother, who is a neuropsychologist, told him he was being "silly." He has had similar problems with getting an official diagnosis and has been told, for example, that he makes too much eye contact to be autistic. Though not an uncommon experience among others interviewed, James's situation may be uniquely impacted by the NHS, which has been documented attempting to cut costs by limiting autism diagnoses to the "most severe cases." He has, regardless, found a lot of support and solidarity from online and in-person autistic groups.

Perhaps surprisingly, given their support of his transition, James's work colleagues have been largely unsupportive of his autism by failing to understand or accommodate his difficulties with navigating workplace social expectations. He is now on disability leave, due to developing chronic fatigue syndrome and fibromyalgia, which he attributes to stress leading up to having top surgery. Unfortunately, this has isolated James from his usual support networks and routine, though he has developed some new friendships through the autism, transgender, and kink communities.

James is a very insightful and deeply contemplative man who has given a lot of thought to the overlap between his experience of autism and gender identity. He finds that, as an autistic person transitioning to male, he wanted to accomplish as binary a transition as possible and found it difficult to accept uncertainty in his own transition. He has also explored the causative relationship between his autism and gender identity and, while he has no firm conclusion on this, regards transition as the right decision for him.

ENDNOTES

1   Baron-Cohen, 2003
2   Baron-Cohen, 2003
3   Wired Staff, 2001
4   Baron-Cohen *et al.*, 2002
5   Russo, 2018
6   Channel 4, 2009
7   FTM London, n.d.
8   TransBareAll, n.d.
9   Vrangalova, 2018
10 Auer *et al.*, 2014
11 Meier *et al.*, 2013
12 Katz-Wise *et al.*, 2016
13 The word stealth refers to a person who is transgender, but is not out as such in their everyday life. In this case, it refers to a transgender man who "passes" as a cisgender man at work.
14 Davis, 2019
15 Draeper, 2017
16 Channel 4, n.d.
17 Kerrigan *et al.*, 2015
18 Cendrowski, 2007

MOOSE

Moose is a Japanese and Korean gay transgender man in his late twenties. Born in Japan, he came to the US as a youth and currently lives in Chicago. Though Moose opted to use his real name, due to his irregular status in the US, we have chosen to obscure some identifying details and employ a pseudonym. He uses he/him pronouns.

COMING OUT AS AUTISTIC

Moose was formally diagnosed with *jiheishou*[1] when he was four years old. His parents rejected the diagnosis (which they saw as shameful to the family name) and sought, without success, to have it removed by five different doctors. They also stopped celebrating his birthday afterwards and, on one occasion, his mother even tried to strangle him. Moose saw this as understandable given their social status and the tendency in Japan at that time to attribute autism to bad parenting, particularly from mothers. He pointed out that there is also a lot of stigma around mental illness in Japan and, more generally, within Asian families.

Moose has had a much more positive experience in Chicago. For instance, though he initially hid his autism from friends after moving there, he ultimately came out both because his symptoms had become too pronounced to hide, due to starting testosterone, and he no longer had the desire to. By contrast,

Moose wasn't able to access autism supports when he was in New Orleans due to "stop and frisk" actions by police that targeted him as a person of colour. This impeded his ability to be "out" about this aspect of his identity.

COMING OUT AS TRANSGENDER

Moose knew he was transgender before he was five years old. His experience is, however, made unique by gendered linguistic characteristics specific to Japanese. For instance, in Japanese there is a specific "I" for boys, girls, teens, and "when males want to appear tough." Moose recalled that he never used the "I" for girls and, even when his teacher called his parents, refused to change his male sentence structure.

Moose's parents initially dismissed this behaviour as a phase. However, his persistence, combined with an inability to navigate the social conventions necessary to hide it, made this untenable. Moose was adamant, for instance, that he would grow a penis when he got older, constantly told his parents he was a boy, and refused to wear the female school uniform, which required a skirt, until junior high. Over time, his parents became concerned that there might be something "mentally wrong with him" and, ultimately, responded to his being different by disowning him.

LINKS BETWEEN AUTISM AND GENDER IDENTITY

Moose feels strongly that gender identity and autism aren't related. He specifies that, while the former establishes what he identifies as, the latter indicates the way in which he processes sensory inputs differently from neurotypicals. Moose indicates that he is not autistic because he is transgender, or transgender because he is autistic, and that his gender identity is not an autistic obsession, as has sometimes been assumed.[2]

Nevertheless, while Moose's autistic symptoms, like rocking, stimming,[3] and echolalia, were present and controllable before starting testosterone, he found that they increased afterwards, leading him to "overload." In particular, his sense of sound, smell, and awareness of his body became much more intense. Moose feels that these changes might be due to interactions between his brain chemistry, autism, and testosterone, but also to having moved to a more accepting city, where he didn't have to suppress his autistic traits as much. While he stims more post transition, he is also more self-confident and less personally inclined to hide his transgender identity or expend effort on hiding autistic traits to please others. In any case, Moose feels that publicly stimming isn't as bad as denying his gender identity. Although his transition caused him to lose the ability to hide his autistic symptoms, he gained the ability to live without shame. In fact, as his body and voice started to match his gender identity, resulting in less misgendering, he experienced less dysphoria and misgendering-related sensory overload.

FAMILY

Moose was formally disowned by his family due to being autistic and transgender when he was a teenager and has not had any contact with them in the many years since. He relates this primarily to his family's cultural heritage and social conservatism due to their samurai lineage. Moose clarifies that, as his father is a first-born son of the main family lineage, his is the root family (本家). As the sole daughter, or "heiress," he was expected to marry a man under the family name and produce another heir or heiress. His autism, and later his transgender identity, were seen as shameful abnormalities that disrupted these plans.

Overall, Moose found his parents to be very exacting, especially academically. He was, for example, beaten with an open hand for A-grades and attacked with fists and stabbed with pens for anything less. As abuse from his mother got worse, Moose, fearing for his safety, sought out overseas academic scholarships as an escape route. He first applied to an exchange program at 11 and since then has attended schools in four different countries. Moose has not been back to Japan in 15 years, though he initially returned for summer vacations.

COMMUNITY AND ACTIVISM

Moose is a Catholic and was very involved in the young adult leadership and board of his local church. He had, in this and other roles, been working to further transgender inclusivity, which resulted in local and national media coverage. Unfortunately, this led his priest to out him, fellow parishioners to send him threatening emails, and he lost a well-paying job.

Moose relates that race was also a factor in preventing his accessing LGBT and autism supports in New Orleans. This was largely because police continuously "stopped and frisked"[4,5] him when he attempted to attend the suburban LGBT centre. Conversely, although he thought the urban LGBT centre might be more welcoming, he was prevented from attending by police officers who told him he wasn't "dark enough" to live in that neighbourhood.

Moose moved to Chicago after his friend noted that it had better access to transgender healthcare, was safer due to LGBT protection laws, and he could access supports there as an Asian. Still, while it takes a somewhat different form, he has continued to experience racism and prejudice. For instance, as a person of colour, Moose was "harassed for three days straight" when Donald Trump was elected and has continued to experience more racism than before "for being Asian and yellow." However, he "felt so lucky that," unlike New Orleans, he could access the LGBT centre without being deterred by police or needing a "white friend to take" him. Moose speculates that this may be because Chicago police are more used to seeing Asians and that he has some privilege as a person with relatively light skin.[6,7]

Since moving to Chicago, Moose has felt safe enough to seek community supports and has become more involved in both the autism and transgender communities. Nevertheless, he has found the autistic community to be very white and, while meetings occur for people of colour, they are rare and tend to take place in restaurants, which he can't afford. Moose's work schedule has also impeded his ability to participate in transgender community groups in person. As a result, he primarily interacts with the autism and transgender communities online, especially on Facebook, where he is the moderator of several groups. Moose also gives talks about autism inclusivity in the transgender community.

Despite being openly autistic on several dating profiles, Moose has found that many people need to be explicitly informed of this and will stop responding when he does so. He worries that being seen as having a developmental disorder or disability leads others to see him as "undateable" and fears that he won't ever find a partner. However, Moose values his independence and, as the autism community has shared with him that love and dating are very difficult, feels that he may be better off without a partner.

WORK

Moose works part-time at a gay bar and full-time in an administrative job. After moving to Illinois, which has strong LGBT anti-discrimination laws, he was able to be openly autistic in job interviews and at work. Moose's experiences with this have been mostly positive, though he finds that people at the bar sometimes talk down to him by speaking slowly or bending down in a patronizing manner, which makes him angry.

By contrast, his full-time job is very understanding and offers accommodations, like turning off fluorescent lighting, while encouraging and supporting him to develop a workplace policy on autism and disability.

HEALTHCARE

Moose has found it much more difficult to access transgender healthcare as someone who is autistic. In fact, one of the reasons he moved to Chicago was because, in his former city, autistic people were subjected to extended gatekeeping, including wait times, before being prescribed hormones.[8] Moose inadvertently subjected himself to this system when he told his doctor he had autism and, as a result, was never able to access testosterone there.

Moose later learned of the extended gatekeeping process for autistic people from other transgender people. When he asked his doctor about it, he couldn't get clarification as to whether it was this practitioner's personal policy or that of the hospital clinic in which he worked. Moose learned only that his doctor attributed it to a need to determine that his gender identity was not an autistic obsession or fixation. However, while intended to protect vulnerable populations, this policy, which pressured him to hide his autism and withheld much-needed transitional healthcare, had the opposite effect. Moose specifically felt that, by prolonging the waiting period for autistics, his doctor failed to care for his gender dysphoria and abandoned the medical oath to "do no harm."

After moving to Chicago, Moose sought healthcare at an LGBT positive clinic, which operates on a sliding payment scale, practices harm reduction, and has expertise in transgender health. As a result of earlier experiences, he didn't tell his doctor about having autism. He received testosterone right after obtaining preliminary blood work, as is the case with neurotypical patients. He later came out to his doctor about having autism and learned that she knew about both his autism and the medical biases against people who are both transgender and autistic in his former city.

It is also important to note that Moose has limited ability to pay for healthcare. While he initially received healthcare coverage through his university, he exhausted his educational savings paying for asthma treatment when it was determined to be a pre-existing condition.[9] This left Moose without enough funds to finish his degree and, as a result, he lost all healthcare coverage. Now, as an undocumented immigrant with no recourse to Medicare or Medicaid,[10] his access to healthcare is limited by his ability to pay for it in cash. Moose cannot afford "top surgery," although he would like to. He has struggled with pressure, in some transmasculine communities, to "pass" and access particular medical procedures. He attributes this tendency to toxic masculinity, immaturity, and the assumption that all procedures are affordable through either personal finances or insurance.

MEDIA REPRESENTATION

Moose identifies several examples of transgender and autistic inclusion in popular media. However, he has never seen someone who is both transgender and autistic represented. Moose explains that, in US media, autism is always portrayed by, and reflected in the experience of, white people. He further explains that (while it may have changed since he was last there) media in Japan tends to reflect what is produced overseas, with similarly little representation of people of colour. A few programs stood out for Moose, however; one in the 21st century about Satoshi Tajiri, who attributed his creation of Pokémon to autism;[11] a YouTube channel about adults with Asperger's in the workplace; and a drama with a neurotypical boy band singer in the role of an autistic person.[12] He disliked the last performance, which he felt was very similar to *Rain Man*.[13]

SOCIAL RULES

While many autistic people have difficulty determining and adjusting to unwritten and unspoken social rules and conventions, Moose's experience as Japanese, transgender, and autistic is unique. This seemed to be especially true with gendered social expectations and rules, as what is considered masculine in Eastern Asian culture isn't always masculine in the US. In Japan, for instance, "endurance in silence" is a central characteristic of masculinity, whereas in the US, vocally "standing your ground" is praised. Moose also notes that, in contrast to the US, Japanese men stand closer together and even talk while at urinals. As a result, he has found that he may appear to be acting feminine in a Western context, while simultaneously performing masculinity in an Eastern one. Moose attributed his being perceived as a feminine gay man to these cultural differences and noted that this can make it harder for him to be perceived as male.

FINAL THOUGHTS

Moose is a Japanese/Korean, gay, transgender man, in his late twenties. Currently living in Chicago, he immigrated to the US from Japan several years ago. While Moose opted to use his real name, because of his irregular immigration status, we have made the decision to protect his identity by using a pseudonym and obscuring some other details.

Moose has experienced a number of obstacles in his path to recognition and self-acceptance as an autistic and transgender man. These include, most notably, if not exhaustively, family rejection, healthcare gatekeeping, and racism. Many of the individuals interviewed for this book share some or all of these concerns. Moose's situation is, however, unique in the manner in which these experiences interact.

Moose's family is the main line of a very traditional Japanese family. As such, his existence, as both autistic and transgender, defies the plans and roles expected of him. Moose's family steadfastly refused to accept either multiple autism diagnoses or his clearly voiced male identity, and ultimately abused and disowned him. His family's exacting standards, particularly regarding academic and social roles, were also mirrored in other interviewees' narratives.

By contrast, once out of Japan, Moose was able to connect with other autistic people and communities, which was critical to both accepting himself as autistic, and accessing care for it. He was similarly able to explore his gender identity, meet others doing so, and decide to transition medically. He did note, however, that the difference between gendered social role expectations in Japan and the US made this process somewhat more complicated. For instance, he is perceived as a feminine gay man in the US for engaging in the same behaviour that is seen as very masculine in Japan.

Moose has experienced a number of barriers in accessing healthcare. As a student in the US, he initially had healthcare insurance through his university; however, he exhausted his educational savings on asthma treatment, after it was classified as a pre-existing condition, and was forced to drop out of school, leaving him completely without insurance. Now, as an undocumented immigrant, he has no access to healthcare beyond what he can pay for out of his own pocket and cannot, therefore, afford more costly procedures like top surgery.

Moose has on several occasions been denied transitional healthcare due to being autistic. This was especially the case in New Orleans, where those with autism were subjected to an extended waiting period, in order to rule out the possibility that their desire to transition was somehow an "autistic fixation." Moose ultimately moved to Chicago, in part to obtain unbiased healthcare, and, in doing so, succeeded in obtaining a prescription for testosterone within the same timeframe as a neurotypical person. Interestingly, he reports that testosterone has made his autistic symptoms more pronounced, limiting his ability to hide them, which he fortunately no longer feels the need to do. In fact, the law in Illinois protects him from discrimination due to race, disability, or gender identity and, as a result, he is able to work as an openly autistic and transgender person.

Moose has also experienced a great deal of racism. While he considers Chicago to be better in this regard, he has been subjected to regular prejudice there since Trump was elected. In New Orleans, however, police prevented him from accessing autism or LGBT supports in the suburbs by "stopping and frisking" and redirecting him because he was not white. He was similarly prevented from attending LGBT services in urban neighbourhoods for being "too light." By contrast, Moose has been able to access autism and transgender community supports in Chicago, although he finds that members of the autism groups, at least, are still largely white.

Moose's life has included a number of hardships, not least in the form of family abuse, racism, and ableism. Nevertheless, while we may be tempted to view Moose's story as largely negative, it is also, above all, a narrative of resilience, self-reliance, and community. In recognizing the need to escape his abusive family situation, and fully realize himself as autistic and transgender, at 11 years old Moose concocted and carried out a plan to apply to successive boarding schools in the US. While this option is clearly not open to everyone, it demonstrates his resourcefulness and self-reliance. Though Moose continues to experience challenges, he also has the support of a wide-reaching network of friends and community and, above all, has found a way to forge his own unique path, regardless of the obstacles in his way.

ENDNOTES

1 The Japanese term for autism.
2 Strang *et al.*, 2018b
3 Short for self-stimulating behaviour, stimming is used by autistics and can consist of repetitive movements like hand flapping, to self-regulate when overwhelmed by sensory input, or purely for enjoyment (Bakan, 2015).
4 Morgan, 2013
5 The Williams Institute, 2015
6 Ramirez, 2018
7 Chen, 2017
8 This is not an uncommon experience (Burns, 2017).
9 In many healthcare insurance regimes, particularly in the US, pre-existing conditions are defined as existing before the onset of insurance coverage, and thus are not paid for.
10 Medicare and Medicaid are US government programs that provide limited medical coverage to people who are over 65, disabled, and/ or on a low income.
11 Eldred-Cohen, 2018
12 Myeong-hong, Seung-yeop, & Chang-hwan, 2005
13 Johnson & Levinson, 1988

NAMI

Nami is a 33-year-old Taiwanese Hakka Han woman living in Toronto, who identifies as asexual/pansexual. Born in Taipei, she has identified as female for as long as she can remember. She first suspected that she was autistic in elementary school and now considers herself part of the larger autistic community. Nami's experience of diagnosis, however, has been murkier and, as a result, she isn't sure whether she currently has an "official" diagnosis of autism. She uses she/her pronouns and has also chosen the pseudonym "Nami."

COMING OUT AS AUTISTIC

Nami first suspected that she was autistic, or, in her words, "broken," around grade three and subsequently received a preliminary autism diagnosis and treatment for autistic symptomology while growing up in Taiwan. She has since received a disorienting number of labels, including high-functioning autism, low-functioning autism, and, now, neurotypical with overlapping autistic-like symptoms due to developmental trauma. This last diagnosis, however, was made informally by a psychiatrist, who is also a close friend.

Nevertheless, Nami claims an autistic identity, which she first took up on entering university. She was, in part, prompted to do so by a transfeminine and autistic friend with whom she felt a strong kinship. Both had a delay between experiencing and processing events, lacked object constancy, and didn't expect regular connection during each other's absence. She describes their friendship as "something frozen that only required defrosting" and, as a result, they were able to pick up their friendship right where they'd left it, despite not having seen or heard from each other since they were children. Nami's understanding of this as an autistic trait helped her to begin to understand herself as autistic,[1] though her psychiatrist has attributed this, and other autistic behaviours, to developmental trauma.

Nami sees herself as part of the Mad Movement which, arising out of the anti-psychiatry movement, rejects and resists over-pathologization of what they view as neurological difference, rather than mental illness.[2] Accordingly, she rejects diagnostic labels that serve no practical purpose and has a general distrust of psychiatric pathologization. Nami likens the Mad Movement's fight to decriminalize mental health to the neurodiversity movement's[3] efforts to de-pathologize autism. She notes that, despite the rise of terms like neuroplasticity,[4] "normalcy" remains the arbitrary standard on which everyone is measured, with those deviating from it seen as "lesser than." Despite this, Nami attests that everyone has autistic traits, making the concept of "normal" impossible, and observes that we would not have science without them.

COMING OUT AS TRANSGENDER

Nami first expressed "crossdressing behaviour" when she was seven years old. Some years later, she mimicked menstruation using her mother's underwear, sanitary products, and red watercolour paint. Nami was largely unaware of transgender people at the time, outside stereotypes of transsexual sex workers, and prejudices about Thai Kathoey[5] workers who performed "vulgar and hypersexualized" shows in Taiwan.

When she was very young, Nami's mother asked her if she wanted to be a girl, and though she very much did, she responded "no." She did so, in part, because she did not wish to emulate her mother who, as the only female member of her family, was her sole example of womanhood. This effectively (if temporarily) halted her exploration of her gender identity. Nevertheless, Nami now realizes that she has, consciously or not, tended to mirror her mother's values and mindset, and wonders whether this might be a reflection of her autism.

Nami's ability to come to terms with her identity as female was further complicated by experiencing years of sexual abuse at the hands of her "uncle."[6] To cope with the trauma, she told herself that only women get assaulted and therefore she must not be a woman. It took her a long time to overcome this internalized misogyny and accept her female identity. In fact, Nami did not come out voluntarily. She had initially planned to commit suicide after her parents passed away, reasoning that, at this point, her duty to them would be at an end, leaving her to "join the ring of reincarnation and maybe have better luck in her next life." Nami's mother's constant criticism, however, led to a different outcome. Her mother relentlessly criticized the way she dressed, as well as her long hair and nails, even taking a sadistic pleasure in cutting them short. This culminated during a family breakfast, while she was home from university, when she was relentlessly interrogated and accused of being gay and dating a man. Nami deliberated on this incident for a few days before deciding to come out as a woman to her family, which they took badly.[7]

Nami observes that her orientation towards transgender diagnosis mirrors her approach to autism in that, unless related to a practical purpose, she doesn't see the need. Unfortunately, without a diagnosis, it is often difficult or impossible for transgender people to move forward with medical and social transition. Nami finds this type of gatekeeping deeply problematic.

LINKS BETWEEN AUTISM AND GENDER IDENTITY

Nami feels that, while there may be a link between transgender
identity and autism, it could result from correlation rather than
causation. They may, for instance, appear connected because
autistic people are inherently more visible due to being less able
to mimic cisgender behaviours or lie about their transgender
identity. More broadly, she wonders whether the neurodiversity
model could be applied to both autism and gender variance.

FAMILY

Nami's mother was very invasive of her privacy and demanding
of her academic and social performance while she was growing
up. She set unreasonably high standards, and when Nami failed
to meet them, Nami was blamed and told to "try harder." Nami
was sent to boarding school in the US at age 12 in an attempt
to improve her academic achievement. Ultimately, her mother
reacted with disapproval and disgust when Nami came out
as female. Nami's revelation of being autistic, though largely
insignificant in the wake of coming out as female, was met with
a similar reaction and the assertion that it wasn't true because
"my son couldn't be such." She knows of no others with autism
in her family, though she understands that it may be heritable.[8]

According to Nami, this is consistent with East Asian
culture, in which children tend to be seen as property and an
investment, rather than human beings with their own sense
of self. She wryly observes, however, that reparative therapy
for transgender children wouldn't be legal[9] in North America
if they didn't share the same perspective. Nevertheless, in the
eyes of her mother, Nami's failure as a son who can carry on
the family name reflects her own social failure. Though she had
until that point managed the family finances, this duty, along
with other privileges and family support, were stripped from

her after coming out as transgender. Her mother's logic is that Nami is a failed investment that she must now sell at a loss.

COMMUNITY AND ACTIVISM
Nami has been more involved with the transgender than the autism community. She has, for instance, participated in programs through Toronto's 519 Community Centre.[10] Nami has also mentored a few autistic people, and worked with the LGBTQ community as both a sexual health educator and advocate, and with migrants seeking refuge in Canada.

WORK
While she is able bodied, Nami considers herself to be less "able minded," which limits her ability to do intense mental work for more than a few days without experiencing severe fatigue and "crashing." This is largely due to her autism, which impairs her ability to multi-task, or interact with others without putting a great deal of effort into anticipating and managing social interactions. Though she worries that it is overly rigid and ineffective, Nami copes, in part, by using social scripts.[11] This strategy enables her to better communicate, reduces her anxiety, and gives her mental space to watch for social cues like blink frequency and changes in facial expression, which is especially difficult, as she experiences facial blindness.[12] Nami notes, for instance, that she isn't able to identify a smile, even if it is very rigid, but that she can "intellectually" register a sudden change from a neutral facial expression to a smile as a positive sign. She is, as a result, extremely capable at tasks that require planning and considered bursts of energy, like event planning and management, but less able to manage a nine-to-five job.

HEALTHCARE

In addition to autism, Nami has a number of degenerative autoimmune disorders, which, fortunately, are currently well managed. Her experience of healthcare has, however, been largely negative. For instance, she recalls that, in elementary school, she was forced to see a counsellor who violated her confidentiality by disclosing the content of their sessions to her mother. This has subsequently impacted her ability to trust healthcare practitioners and, in particular, mental healthcare providers.

Though she has never been subjected to ABA, the treatment that she did undergo for autistic symptomology was traumatic nevertheless. As a child, she experienced difficulty with small muscle control and hand–eye coordination, which made it difficult for her to perform tasks like balancing or catching a ball. Nami's therapist proposed to treat issues like poor balance by prescribing exercises where she practiced moving along the ground while lying face down on a board. While it was intended to be an indoor activity, her mother moved it outside, requiring Nami to brake the momentum of the board while it went down the steep hills near their home.

Nami's parents felt comfortable modifying the therapists' treatment protocols because they both worked in the healthcare field, though neither possessed any expertise in occupational therapy or autism. They believed that they would be able to achieve better and faster success by making the exercises more difficult, but only succeeded in risking Nami's health, and causing her mental and physical trauma. In fact, in the process, she sustained a number of physical injuries and even, by her description, near death experiences. Nami sees this as reckless and perhaps intentionally malicious. While she acknowledges that the prescribed therapy helped to some extent, particularly in fine motor skills like holding a pencil, the constant pressure from her parents pushed her into a "failure narrative."

Nami reflects that she is not very in tune with her emotions and has, for as long as she can remember, experienced dissociation. As a result, her emotions are often isolated from the world around her, and she must put a great deal of effort and intention into thinking, reading, and planning for social interactions. Nami's demeanour, while outwardly apathetic, hides a wealth of emotions; however, her experience of them is often delayed, sometimes by weeks or even months. She also intentionally uses "thick skin" as a coping mechanism to deal with dissociation and the world around her.

Nami isn't usually aware of being treated differently by healthcare practitioners for her female identity or autism, though largely because she fails to notice, rather than a lack of discrimination. When she does notice, it is because the incident has become very obvious, in which case, her female identity is usually the point of contention. Nami relayed one incident in which she saw a Chinese eye specialist in Scarborough for rheumatic iritis. During this visit, her transgender history was announced in the waiting room and the doctor asked when she would be having "the surgery."

MEDIA REPRESENTATION

Nami hasn't seen her own experiences reflected in popular media. She declined to comment on autistic-only representation. Nami did address transgender-only representation, though only to note that she finds it strange that transgender roles are usually filled by cisgender actors.

SOCIAL RULES

Nami studies social situations as if they were textbooks, analyzing every possible scenario, and predicting outcomes. She sees this as typical of transfeminine individuals, who may seek to avoid conflict, due to the extraordinary degree of transphobic violence they face.[13,14] Nami largely passes as female now and, as such, doesn't really experience confusion from others as to what social role she should fill. However, she shared that people sometimes respond with violence when she does fail to pass. Nami relayed a story from about 2011 in which she was approached by a white man in his early twenties outside a subway station. The man approached her from behind and tapped on her shoulder while she was on the phone. Nami turned around and asked if she could help him and the man, whose face "turned red," started pointing at her and yelling "You are a man, you are a fucking man!" She was able to extract herself from the situation by staying on her phone while quickly turning around and walking away but worries that it could have turned out much worse. Nami shared that this is one of the reasons why she always exerts a lot of effort to pass as female.

FINAL THOUGHTS

Nami is a 33-year-old Hakka Han woman who was born in Taiwan and currently lives in Toronto. She has had a dizzying array of neurodevelopmental diagnoses following a prospective diagnosis of autism as a young child in Taiwan and, though she was recently informally diagnosed as "not autistic," continues to see herself as part of the autistic community. As a result, Nami aligns herself with the Mad Movement, in "defying diagnosis," and the neurodiversity movement, in seeing autism as a natural human variation. Her approach to transgender diagnosis and gatekeeping is similarly influenced.

Nami first started "crossdressing" when she was very young, but her ability to further explore her gender identity at that time was cut short by a lack of positive transgender or female role models. In fact, though she has always "felt female," she did not intend to come out. Rather, she had planned to kill herself after her parents passed away. It was only when her parents forced her out of the closet that she began to fully explore and accept her gender identity. Her parents, however, did not react positively and were not supportive of either her autism or gender identity. Nami's experience here parallels Moose's (in the previous chapter), in that both come from Asian families that demanded they perform beyond their capacities, sent them to US boarding schools when attempts to "fix" their autism failed, and rejected them completely as transgender. Nami relates this to her view that East Asian culture sees children as property and an investment.

Nami recounted a number of negative healthcare experiences. Those that stand out include ethics violations from medical specialists and therapists and her parents' dangerous modification of autism treatment protocols. These incidents have understandably made it difficult for Nami to approach and trust medical professionals. Nevertheless, Nami is resilient. She is very active in the transgender and autistic communities, even acting as a mentor to other autistic people on several occasions. Nami has also contributed to the LGBTQ community as a sexual health educator and an advocate for queer migrants. While autism (in particular, facial blindness) sometimes makes this difficult, her experiences have taught her to manage anxiety and communication by studying social situations closely and using social scripts. Nami has also found that autism makes her a uniquely capable event planner and, overall, her experiences have helped her to develop a valuable criticism of psychiatry and pathologization.

ENDNOTES

1   Bertilsdotter Rosqvist, Brownlow, & O'Dell, 2015
2   Jackson, 2013
3   Crow, 2017

4   "A general umbrella term that refers to the brain's ability to modify, change, and adapt both structure and function throughout life and in response to experience" (Voss *et al.*, 2017, p.1).

5   A culturally specific gender identity, broadly comparable to "transgender woman," used in Thailand (Winter, 2006).

6   In Chinese and Taiwanese culture, older friends of the family are often referred to as uncle or aunt.

7   Nami doesn't strictly identify as transgender. Her general stance is that gender is and should be respected as self-declared.

8   Autism does, in fact, appear to be highly heritable (Sandin *et al.*, 2017), with recent large-scale research demonstrating that 80 percent is inherited (Bai *et al.*, 2019).

9   Parallels with treatments for autistics should also be drawn here, as with the Judge Rotenberg Center in Massachusetts, US, which uses powerful electric shocks to control the behaviour of autistic children (Pilkington, 2018).

10   The 519 Community Centre, n.d.

11   Social scripts are a strategy where a person develops and uses set responses to typical questions and scenarios. They are also sometimes referred to as "social stories" or "comic strip conversations" (National Autistic Society, 2018).

12   Formally known as prosopagnosia, and not uncommon among those with autism, it denotes the inability to recognize faces (Davis, 2006).

13   Perry & Dyck, 2014

14   Human Rights Campaign, n.d.

NATHAN

Nathan is a 26-year-old queer and transgender man from Houston, Texas, of Black and multiracial (white, native) heritage. He currently manages the Transgender Health Lab at the University of Houston, and has a formal diagnosis of autism. Nathan has opted to use his real name and uses he/him pronouns.

COMING OUT AS AUTISTIC

Nathan first suspected that he was autistic in 2011. He was, at the time, a regular watcher of the shows *Parenthood*[1] and *Degrassi*,[2] both of which have characters with Asperger's, and subsequently became interested in reading more on the subject. He chanced on the book *Look Me in the Eye*, by John Elder Robinson,[3] which he found closely described his own experiences. Nathan was then prompted to talk with his mother about the possibility of being autistic. He largely kept his suspicions to himself until late 2017, when he chose to discuss some executive functioning difficulties with his employer, who, as a clinical psychologist, had suspected Nathan was autistic and was waiting for him to disclose this on his own.

Executive function refers to the capacity to self-regulate and direct behaviours towards a goal. It allows us "to break our habits, make decisions and evaluate risks, plan for the future, prioritize and sequence our actions, and cope with novel situations."[4] Though investigations into the incidence of executive dysfunction in autistics are mixed, many studies do demonstrate a significant and consistent impairment in this area.[5]

Nathan has had difficulty obtaining a formal diagnosis. His psychologist initially "shut him down" when he brought it up, because Nathan didn't fit his image of a person with autism, which prompted him to stop seeing this professional for a period. Nathan only recently started seeing this psychologist again after he committed to learn more about autism and explore the issue with him. Despite worrying that he might appear to be taking something away from or invalidating those with a diagnosis, Nathan is nonetheless largely at peace with not having one.[6] This is, in part, because the school and work accommodations that might help him are typically only available to those who received a diagnosis prior to age 16.

COMING OUT AS TRANSGENDER

Nathan first came out to himself as transgender in March 2010. He was, at the time, attending a transgender support group as part of a senior project during his last semester of high school. Nathan described how he deeply identified with aspects of other participants' "gender journeys" and, as with autism, "something just clicked." In terms of coming out, he first tested the waters by asking friends, "What would you think if I said I was really a guy?" Nathan subsequently spoke with his school therapist and told his friends that he did, in fact, identify as a man. He informed his family last. Overall, Nathan characterizes his coming out experience as "pretty smooth."

LINKS BETWEEN AUTISM AND GENDER IDENTITY

When asked, Nathan indicated that he didn't feel that autism and gender identity were intrinsically related, though they can share common factors and influence each other, depending on the person. For instance, his autism impaired his ability to pick up on unspoken gender norms and rules and, ultimately, to evade female socialization. Nathan related that it also influences how he interacts with the world as a man. Though he is intellectually aware of the clothing expectations for men, he nevertheless chooses to select clothes according to his own preference and comfort, and without regard to gender.

FAMILY

Nathan's family has largely been supportive of both his autism and gender identity. As regards his gender identity, the first person he came out to in his family was his oldest brother, whom he felt would be supportive as a gay man. In fact, though his brother eventually came to accept it, he initially "questioned it quite a bit." Nathan then wrote a coming out letter to his parents. He describes their reaction as "not unsupportive," and primarily characterized by needing time to process the information. Nathan's parents now attend all the events he organizes and volunteers at and "are as involved in the transgender community as [he] is."

Overall, Nathan's parents are also accepting of his autism, though they have had difficulty reconciling their need to show physical affection with his for limited physical contact. This has been particularly difficult for his father. His mother is more understanding in this regard, possibly due to her long career in special education and psychology. She does, nevertheless, find it difficult not to share physical affection with him, especially since they are quite close. Nathan also shared that his mother may be broadly autistic and, according to her, his grandmother likely was.

COMMUNITY AND ACTIVISM

Nathan is very active as both a participant and organizer in the transgender community. For instance, he manages the University of Houston's Transgender Health Lab[7] and helps to organize an annual conference, called Gender Infinity,[8] for transgender youth and their parents. With regards to the latter, Nathan has worked hard to increase programs for people of colour, Spanish speakers, and those who are disabled.

More recently, Nathan has used his skills to address issues important to the transgender and autistic community. He is, for example, currently working on research which challenges other publications[9] that posit that "transgender men…are just autistic women who [became masculinized because they] weren't able to socialize with female peers." To date, Nathan has presented this research at the Philadelphia Transgender Wellness Conference[10] and at the biannual conference of the World Professional Association for Transgender Health (WPATH) in Buenos Aires, Argentina.[11]

WORK

As noted, Nathan manages the Transgender Health Lab at the University of Houston, which has undertaken a longitudinal investigation into the mental health impacts of testosterone on transgender men[12] and investigated the impacts of social transition on youth.[13] The lab is heavily involved in the transgender community and the creation of transgender health-related infographics. As part of his duties, Nathan has presented their research at both the 2018 WPATH and Gender Infinity conferences.

HEALTHCARE

In addition to autism, Nathan is diagnosed with generalized anxiety disorder (GAD), OCD, agoraphobia, hoarding, and chronic migraines, which he characterizes as symptoms or traits of his autism. When seeking healthcare, he goes either to Houston's main transgender healthcare provider or to the private practice of a doctor recommended through word of mouth as competent in transgender healthcare. Overall, and despite his psychologist's initial dismissal of his autism, he sees his healthcare experience as uneventful.

Nathan receives a number of disability-related educational accommodations. These include (but are not limited to) priority seating near the exit, supplemental class notes, an allowance for greater absences, increased exam time, and permission to record lectures. There is no official channel for receiving accommodations in his workplace, but he has found that they make a point of supporting people in whatever way is needed.

Nathan wants people, especially those who are autistic and transgender, to know that autism doesn't preclude being transgender, or vice versa. Nevertheless, those who wish to medically transition may need to consider things that neurotypicals do not, like the need to articulate and present gender in a manner accessible to neurotypical healthcare professionals. Some will also need to navigate challenges to their capacity to decide on and direct transitional healthcare. Nathan recommends that transgender and autistic people fight the temptation to internalize these barriers.

MEDIA REPRESENTATION

Nathan has seen media representations of transgender and autistic people separately, but never in the same person, or central to the plot. He notes that while there are many characters who are coded as autistic, it is not usually explicitly stated, and that negative or biased portrayals can influence public misconceptions about autistic people. Nevertheless, Nathan feels that as visibility has grown, transgender people are increasingly being presented positively and even given more opportunities to play these roles themselves.

SOCIAL RULES

Nathan is grateful that his autism made him somewhat impervious to gender role expectations growing up. He tries to acknowledge this privilege by undermining those expectations whenever he can. Nathan also commented extensively on how the unique cultural and social expectations in the Black community impacted him as an autistic person—for instance, that these cultural expectations, which in some cases are borne out of racism, can mask and provide an alternative explanation for autistic symptomatology. One example Nathan gave was the prizing of cleanliness as a response to the historically racist perception that Black people are unclean. As a result, obsession with cleanliness might be seen as positive, rather than a symptom of OCD. Similarly, Nathan described how the Black community's emphasis on respect, especially for one's elders, may lead some to see autistic behaviour as defiance. He adds that, "since physical punishment is still seen as acceptable in a lot of communities of colour, adults may believe they can whip it out of their kids." Nathan himself is often seen as rude or disrespectful within Black communities and, as a result, tends to avoid conversations with Black elders he doesn't know.

FINAL THOUGHTS

Nathan is a 26-year-old queer, transgender man, of Black and multiracial heritage. His experience as an autistic person is deeply entwined with his experience as a Black man from the southern United States. As the manager of a transgender research lab at a major university, Nathan also has a unique perspective on the topic and the ability to pursue research on the intersection of transgender and autistic experiences.

Nathan's exposure to autistic characters on television, and the published narratives of autistics, had a big impact on his recognition of himself as autistic. In the same vein, his participation in transgender community groups, as an observer for a school project, led him to an awareness of himself as a transgender man. Nathan observes that while gender identity and autism are not intrinsically related, they can share common factors and influence each other. In his case, the latter may have impacted his ability to pick up on and internalize female socialization.

Nathan's experiences of coming out, first as transgender and then autistic, have been somewhat different. For instance, in coming out as transgender, he first tested the waters by asking friends what they would do if he said he was and, with the support of the school counsellor, proceeded to inform them that this was the case. Nathan told his family last and, while they initially had some difficulty accepting this information, they have since become big supporters. His parents in particular never miss one of the transgender community events he organizes or volunteers at.

Nathan took a somewhat different tack when he came out as autistic. He initially broached the topic with his parents who, while accepting and supportive, had difficulty understanding and respecting his need for minimal physical contact. Otherwise, Nathan largely kept this information to himself until 2017, when he told his employer because he needed workplace accommodations. To his surprise, his boss, a clinical psychologist, had already intuited that he was autistic. Nathan ultimately received a formal autism diagnosis after his psychologist committed to research and explore the issue with him having previously refused to entertain the possibility.

Nathan has several physical and mental health diagnoses that he sees as symptoms of autism. He has two local options for competent and supportive transgender healthcare and has successfully negotiated disability accommodations at both his workplace and school. As a result, he describes his healthcare experience in largely positive terms. Nevertheless, Nathan cautions that other transgender autistics may need to be strategic in articulating their gender identity in a way that is legible to neurotypical professionals and consider how they would navigate challenges to their decision-making capacity. He notes that it can be difficult for people not to internalize this.

As an autistic Black man, Nathan has a unique perspective on the role that social rules and expectations have played in his life, both individually and culturally. He notes, for instance, that respect is highly emphasized in Black southern communities and that, as an autistic man, he is sometimes seen as rude, or disrespectful, especially by elders. Nathan posits that his community may tend to see autistic behaviour as indicative of defiance and respond with physical punishment. His personal response to this is to limit interactions with Black elders that he doesn't know. Similarly, Nathan finds that his cleanliness-related OCD symptoms tend to be seen as positive in the Black community, which he attributes to the historically racist stereotype that they are unclean.

ENDNOTES

1   Howard *et al.*, 2010
2   Schuyler, Stohn, & Yorke, 2002
3   Robinson, 2007
4   Craig *et al.*, 2016, p.1191
5   Demetriou *et al.*, 2017

6   Nathan ultimately received a diagnosis of autism spectrum disorder from his psychologist a few weeks after our interview. Autism is now his primary diagnosis, with his others listed as symptoms.

7   Keo-Meier, n.d.

8   Gender Infinity Conference, n.d.

9   Jones *et al.*, 2012

10 Philadelphia Transgender Wellness Conference, n.d.

11 World Professional Association for Transgender Health, n.d.

12 Meier *et al.*, 2011

13 Ehrensaft *et al.*, 2018

REYNARD

Reynard is a 26-year-old, Afro-Caribbean and Slovenian, gender-queer and non-binary individual. Born in Germany, they previously lived in Alabama, before moving to Chicago, where they currently reside. Reynard was formally diagnosed with autism in their first year of college and is now deeply involved in both the transgender and autistic communities. They have opted to be identified by their real name. They use they/them pronouns.

COMING OUT AS AUTISTIC

Reynard always knew they "weren't on the same wavelength" as other people. However, without the language to identify why, or an awareness that others might have similar struggles, they were isolated. Reynard's differences were, nevertheless, clear to the adults around them. For instance, they had difficulty with inflection, reading, and making facial expressions. In fact, Reynard's teachers would sometimes remark on their similarity to autistic relatives, though they unfortunately never considered this a diagnostic possibility.

While Reynard's regular teachers developed an understanding and even affection for their quirks, without an official diagnosis, they were vulnerable when faced with unfamiliar instructors. To substitute teachers, for example, they sounded "too smart" to be confused and their many questions were seen as an act of defiance and disruption. This issue was exacerbated by the fact that, because Reynard is Black, they were viewed as "prone to intentionally disrupting the class."

Reynard mentioned one case in which a substitute teacher called the school resource officer (SRO)[1] on him. As they recalled, she ran out of copies of a test and, when given the last copy, Reynard offered it to another student who had trouble with the subject and needed more time. This instructor then accused them of refusing to take the test and demanded that they start immediately. When Reynard tried to explain that they couldn't start until more copies were made, she told them "not to tell her what to do" and asked "if [they] thought she was stupid." She ultimately alleged to the SRO that Reynard had attempted to "incite a riot" and, though it was cleared up by teachers familiar with them, it could have gone disastrously wrong.[2] They are acutely aware that, had they been diagnosed earlier, oppositional defiance disorder, or a similar conduct-based disorder, would have been likely due to their race.[3,4,5]

Reynard also recalled the case of Charles Kinsey, in which the African-American behavioural therapist of a Puerto-Rican autistic man was shot by police, because they mistook the autistic man's toy truck for a firearm.[6,7] Reynard worries that, in a situation like this, they or a friend would be shot because they wouldn't be able to explain or understand police instructions quickly enough. Reynard has even practiced looking and sounding non-threatening in anticipation of just such an event. They are, furthermore, aware that their race gives them less leeway in this type of misunderstanding and that protective measures taken by other (white) autistic people aren't practical for them. For instance, there are cards autistic people can use to explain their autism to police,[8] some of which are developed and endorsed by individual states.[9] Reynard doesn't bother with these, however, "because [as a Black, masculine person, they] don't feel safe reaching into [their] pocket for anything around police."

Reynard stumbled across a diagnostic inventory for autism while researching ADHD in their senior year of high school. In fact, ADHD and autism share symptoms, such as difficulty with organization, and executive dysfunction, and there is some evidence of a link between them.[10] Reynard's first reaction on reading about autism was an immediate recognition of its similarity to their own difficulties. Still, they found it hard to accept that they were autistic and not "just weird" due to early childhood trauma, and the fact that their parents came from two different cultures.

Reynard had a neuropsychiatric evaluation in their first year of college, at which they received a diagnosis of autism, despite going in for an ADHD assessment. They recall the process as affirming and helpful, in spite of their concerns and self-doubts, and felt fortunate to have had a diagnostician specialized in autism. Reynard worried, for instance, that their autistic symptoms resulted from being a person who was fundamentally bad or dangerous. The specialist confirmed that they were "definitely on the spectrum" and assured them that it was a natural human variation that was not intrinsically negative. In particular, he highlighted that Reynard's difficulties often resulted from living in a world that isn't designed for people who think like they do, which is more a reflection on society than them. In the end, they found the diagnosis helped to validate and learn to trust their manner of understanding and interacting with the world.

Reynard almost immediately informed their close friends and family about this diagnosis and found them to be affirming and supportive. It was their larger social circle that, owing to inaccurate assumptions and stereotypes about autism, had the most trouble understanding and accepting this information. Some people, for instance, couldn't reconcile the fact that Reynard is highly verbal with the popular stereotype of autistics as totally disabled.

COMING OUT AS TRANSGENDER

Reynard recalls being gender non-conforming as a child. They, for instance, experimented with gender neutral names, were elated when people mistook them for a boy, played middle linebacker in middle school, and insisted on singing tenor in choir. Despite this, Reynard had difficulty seeing themselves as transgender, because it was a term associated, in their mind, with media stereotypes of "men who wore their wives' underwear."

Autism is, of course, a condition characterized by difficulty generalizing from singular examples to broad categories.[11] It may be, therefore, that autistics have difficulty connecting their experience to the larger transgender community because of singular and often misleading, or downright inaccurate, media representation. Some autistic people do, nevertheless, experience gender dysphoria and identify as transgender.

For Reynard, everything fell into perspective when they met a transgender man at age 20. Prior to this, they assumed that their attraction to women mandated that they be a lesbian. Still, Reynard had a hard time separating their sensory issues from gender dysphoria and in deciding to transition. They also worried that they weren't "trans enough," or that hormone therapy would make them sexist and abusive. Nevertheless, Reynard described being intensely dysphoric about their voice, name, and lack of body hair, and deeply resentful of how uncomfortable and disruptive menstruation was. They also once told their father that, "if I grew breasts, I would hack them off with a rusty spoon."

Reynard's best friend Jose, who is an autistic transgender man they describe as very pragmatic, helped put these concerns into perspective. Jose reasoned that, while transition might have downsides, it was an acceptable option if it had more positive than negative outcomes on balance. Jose argued that Reynard had no obligation to be miserable, it wasn't helping anyone, and that hormonal therapy was capable of addressing all the aspects of gender dysphoria that made them most uncomfortable. He helped them understand that they could be whatever kind of transgender person they wanted, which didn't preclude them from wearing dresses, or oblige them to become misogynistic. Reynard considered this and reasoned that no medications or treatments can make someone cisgender and, even if they could, the required brain surgery or medication would still alter their body. They ultimately concluded that their gender identity is foundational to their perception and experience of the world and that, while some aspects of transition might be unpleasant, the positive ones were, on balance, likely to outweigh them.

LINKS BETWEEN AUTISM AND GENDER IDENTITY

Reynard, when asked what they would say to someone who argues that autism caused or impaired their ability to determine their gender identity, responded that this is neither true nor relevant to their life. They reasoned that, while autism may make them more aware of and inclined to question where their gender identity and other aspects of their being diverge from the mainstream, it also makes them less vulnerable to distress resulting from being seen as different. Reynard explained that their transgender identity, even if a manifestation of autism, isn't going to disappear and that, in any case, there is no harm in being transgender, since they "don't kidnap people at the bus stop to acquire new clothes…or harvest testosterone like some kind of hormonal vampire."

FAMILY

Reynard's father is Afro-Caribbean and their mother is Slovenian. While their father and brother are largely supportive of them, their mother, who they describe as "cartoonishly racist," is not. Growing up, Reynard's mother physically and emotionally abused them for both being autistic, which she interpreted as defiance and willfulness, and "too Black." She attributed all Reynard's "good" characteristics, like compassion and precociousness, to their white heritage and their "bad" traits, such as stubbornness, to their Black heritage. As a result, Reynard has chosen not to keep in contact with their mother, and she is not aware of their autism or gender identity.

By contrast, their father has been very supportive of their autism, though their extended family sees it as odd and due to "either being part white or around white people." Nevertheless, Reynard has a cousin who has been diagnosed as autistic, and suspects that other family members are also "on the spectrum." Their father has also been quite supportive of their gender identity, though their first response, when told, was "but that's so expensive!" Reynard countered that there are coupons for medication and describes their father as affable about it since.

Reynard's siblings are very supportive of their gender identity as well. Their sister, for example, is very good about using their chosen name and pronouns. They also relayed an extremely moving story about their brother: Reynard explained that, when they were born female, their parents gave the name chosen for them to their brother and, when they came out, they told him they wanted it back. Amazingly, their brother agreed without hesitation and proceeded to consider potential new names for himself. Although they and their brother ultimately did not pursue this arrangement, it was a deeply touching gesture to Reynard.

COMMUNITY AND ACTIVISM

Reynard moved from Alabama to Chicago specifically so that they could connect with other people in the transgender and autistic communities. They chose Chicago in part for its accessible transit infrastructure; Reynard explained that, in Atlanta, the transit system was such that they had to walk to get most places, which restricted their ability to attend community events. It also made them more reliant on abusive people for transportation. In Chicago, by contrast, Reynard can rely on the transit system to enable them to find and maintain friendships across a wider geographic and socio-economic area. They also appreciate Chicago's diversity and variety, which has allowed them to find their niche while avoiding being tokenized.

Reynard has, since moving to Chicago, volunteered as a patient advocate for transgender and autistic individuals. They accompany people to medical appointments and the emergency room, help them understand paperwork, make sure they aren't misgendered, and assist in translating concerns into language understood and respected by doctors. Reynard also moderates a non-binary and genderqueer discussion group, in which more than half the participants are on the autism spectrum.[12] They support autistic participants, in part, by using social stories[13] to break down the steps in navigating, for instance, doctor's appointments and pronouns at job interviews. Using these and other strategies, Reynard has helped the group develop a number of working agreements.

Reynard explained that they took over the group from previous moderators who were burned out by its dysfunctional nature. At the time, participants didn't feel comfortable setting or enforcing boundaries, and several struggled with social skills. Many continued to attend, however, because they lacked other options. Reynard described the group as an "anxiety engine, eating people up and spitting them out."

Reynard felt that, because their autism led them to learn social skills manually and granularly, it was easier for them to advocate for and explain the structure that should be added to the group. The first change they made was to begin meetings by having participants discuss their "highs and lows" for the week;

that is, something nice and something bad that happened. Reynard quickly discovered that the person with the most intense low got the most attention, which caused others to describe increasingly traumatic events, and distressed the whole group. As a result, they instead started the group by asking participants a silly question, such as "What did you do (or not do) this week that you deserve a sticker for?" Reynard found that this encouraged people to ask for praise in a healthier and more manageable way and, when sharing positive and negative experiences, to emphasize effort over accomplishment.

The group also used to have a rule called "Step up, step up!" to encourage members who frequently talked to listen more and vice versa. Reynard explained that it tended to target people on the spectrum unfairly, however, because it required them to pick up cues that they were speaking too much and caused the group to resent them when they couldn't. The rule also led some group members to over-police themselves and refrain from speaking at all. Reynard, in recognizing that autistic group members needed to have specific, measurable standards to follow, replaced it with a practice where, if a person talks too much, the moderator simply tells them so. The individual is then asked to wait for three people to speak before they do ("three and then me"). Reynard explained that this incident was indicative of a basic difference between autistic and neurotypical people, which is that the latter are culturally primed to avoid direct confrontation, and the former prefer telling people to "shut up when they talk too much."

Reynard offered an interesting example of how these changes helped participants deal with anxiety and bigotry. They were once asked whether being the only person of colour in the group made them lonely or uncomfortable. They noted that this made the neurotypical group members very uncomfortable, which wasn't productive and, for Reynard, clarified that the autistic member had only verbalized what others were already thinking, but were unable to say. They noted that they couldn't work together to fix the situation, or identify the things that made them uncomfortable, if everyone couldn't talk about it openly. The group consists now, as a result of having this conversation, of one-third people of colour.

This incident also caused Reynard to realize that, among European Americans, respect is expressed by "mincing and couching [words, and] deliberately and fastidiously" packaging information in a way that is tiresome for autistics. By contrast, among other Black people, they are encouraged to speak firmly, directly, and proudly, while showing deference through making sure that they enunciate words and are clearly understood. Reynard explains that, in the Black community, it is considered "disrespectful to imply [we] need our words cut up for us into smaller and less heavy pieces, like a toddler's dinner."

HEALTHCARE

Reynard has a number of diagnoses, including autism, ADHD, and anxiety. They are guarded in interactions with healthcare professionals and typically only see doctors when they have something they can't manage on their own. Reynard is careful to prepare for meetings with healthcare professionals ahead of time by researching and preparing a list of concerns and answers to doctor's questions. With the exception of their physical and transitional healthcare, which they recently consolidated under a single trusted provider, they tend to keep their transgender, autistic, and mental health-related care separate from each other.

Reynard keeps their healthcare compartmentalized like this because they are aware of several cases where providers have denied transitional healthcare to people with autism. As a result, they opted to access testosterone therapy through a harm-reduction clinic and were careful not to mention their autism. Reynard also didn't mention their transgender identity when they went to the hospital with a broken arm. Similarly, they have only disclosed their autism with their most recent therapist, for fear of being dismissed as "too verbal" to be autistic. Nevertheless, they describe their experience with healthcare as "fine," and are more concerned about being profiled for seeking unneeded pain medication due to race.

Reynard is very involved in helping his best friend Jose, who is autistic, transgender, quadriplegic, and non-verbal, advocate for and obtain better healthcare. Reynard observes that Jose is especially vulnerable in hospital, because staff there lack knowledge or training in his method of non-verbal communication. They also find that a great deal of advocacy is needed to ensure Jose's gender identity and transitional healthcare needs are respected in hospital. For instance, he is often denied testosterone as an inpatient, though he has an ongoing prescription for it. On another occasion, Reynard had to explain to a nurse that Jose, as a transgender man, could not use a urinal in bed. The nurse then told them, in a conversational manner, that "if her child told her he was trans, she would have preferred that he had died at birth." On other occasions, healthcare practitioners have asked Reynard, as Jose's "service human," whether his quadriplegia is related to being transgender and, even when he is in distress due to choking and in need of immediate assistance, have demonstrated a fixation on what his genitals look like. As a Black transmasculine person, they often have to balance attempts to intervene and advocate for Jose against the need to appear calm and non-threatening, as Jose would be left unassisted if security were called on them.

Reynard explained that Jose is firmly against being admitted to a 24-hour facility due to his sensitivities with sound and light, and a dislike of strangers touching him. As a man who uses adult diapers, he is particularly disturbed by the idea of having strangers "stare at his crotch, while he's helpless to defend himself." Reynard concludes that, because Jose has "enough healthcare problems for both of them and several others," their own are minor by comparison. They observe that the two of them "three-legged race into some measure of functional adulthood," because while Jose is profoundly impacted by autism and thus infantilized, Reynard is high functioning, and therefore overestimated.

MEDIA REPRESENTATION

Reynard wasn't able to connect with other transgender and autistic people until they moved to Chicago. As a result, most of their initial understanding of the community came from movies and TV shows, as well as books and internet forums. In particular, they loved the movie *Mozart and the Whale*.[14]

SOCIAL RULES

Reynard points out that, though their brains work differently, neurotypical perceptions tend to be forced on autistics. For instance, it is presumed and even insisted on that hugs and back rubs must feel good, when this is not the case for many autistic people. To Reynard, this is akin to gaslighting, not least because neurotypical social rules and conventions are often arbitrary and change in unexpected and unpredictable ways. For instance, the Black community favours directness and clarity, and sees Reynard as reserved; conversely, white people prefer indirectness and obfuscation, and see them as aggressive and loud. Code-switching[15] like this, particularly for an autistic person, can be exhausting.

In practical terms, Reynard has a lot of difficulty navigating social rules and expectations. They are, for instance, "embarrassingly prone to getting sexually assaulted," because people read consent into their inability to pick up social cues and relay their intent. Reynard describes one incident in which they agreed to let a person lie in their lap because they didn't objectively see the harm. This escalated to more obviously intimate behaviour, which they didn't consent to, but also didn't know how to signal not being interested in. Reynard takes longer to process information because they are autistic, and, by the time they consider what is happening, their response, and the potential for negative outcomes, the other person might escalate their behaviour, causing them to repeat the cycle of analyzing and processing.

Reynard has responded by developing a list of sexual situations in which they "whitelist" actions. For example, consent is not automatically given, and no one is allowed to get close to them until they have finished processing the situation. Reynard usually feels more comfortable in overtly sexual situations, in which subtlety and non-verbal social cues don't play a part, like gay cruising. In this example, sustained eye contact is clearly coded as an easy-to-decline interest in sex. Bondage/discipline, domination/submission, sadism/masochism (BDSM) communities, which are "high protocol" and have a lot of "structure," are similar. Reynard admits, however, that listing all their desires ahead of time can sometimes make them feel fragile and as if there is no room for improvisation. The inconsistency in their tactile and sensory needs can also be frustrating as, for instance, hugging might be okay on some days and not on others.

FINAL THOUGHTS

Reynard is a 26-year-old mixed-race genderqueer and non-binary person living in Chicago. Diagnosed with autism as an adult, their experience of transgender and autistic healthcare has been largely positive, though they have been careful to separate the healthcare they receive, so that different practitioners are unaware of each other, or their various diagnoses. Reynard has found that, as an autistic person, this is often a necessity to receive access to transitional care. They also worry that healthcare professionals will accuse them of being too verbal to be autistic, which is, in fact, a common concern among those we interviewed. As a result, Reynard tends to avoid doctors and manage their own healthcare and, when this is not possible, carefully prepare for appointments ahead of time.

Overall, Reynard is happy with the healthcare they receive as a transgender and autistic person and is far more concerned about being profiled due to race. They are also very involved in advocating for their friend Jose, who is autistic, transgender, quadriplegic, and non-verbal, and see their own challenges as relatively minor in comparison. In fact, it was Jose who inspired Reynard to transition.

Reynard is far more frustrated by their experiences with social rules and conventions. As a mixed-race person of colour, they often find themselves straddling the equally incomprehensible social expectations of Black and white communities. Reynard relates, for instance, that their Black relatives tend to see them as reserved, while the white community interprets their behaviour as loud and aggressive, and that the former interprets respect as explicitness and directness, while the latter defines it as couching beliefs and feelings in subterfuge. This has, in fact, caused serious and potentially dangerous conflicts with white authority.

Reynard has also found that they are "embarrassingly prone to getting sexually assaulted" because people read consent into their actions, they have difficulty communicating sexual and romantic intent non-verbally, and experience a lag between receiving and processing other people's actions. Additionally, they find that neurotypical romantic preferences and expectations tend to be forced on autistics, such as the assumption that back rubs must feel good, which they experience as a subtle form of gaslighting. Reynard has, as a result, established firm rules around what situations they are comfortable with, which purposefully exclude uncertainty. They are, for instance, more comfortable in "high protocol" spaces, like gay cruising and BDSM communities.

Reynard has a mixed relationship with their family. Their father and brother, for instance, have been overwhelmingly supportive, while their mother is "cartoonishly racist." Reynard has, like many of those interviewed, found critical solidarity and support from the autistic and transgender communities, particularly in Chicago, which they moved to for its greater diversity and transit options. They volunteer as a patient advocate for people who are transgender and autistic and moderate a discussion group for people who are genderqueer and non-binary, where many of the participants are also autistic.

ENDNOTES

1 SROs are law enforcement officers assigned to elementary and high schools, primarily in the United States, but also in Canada and other countries.
2 SRO programs tend to disproportionately target minority and, in particular, Black students.
3 Mandell *et al.*, 2007
4 Maddox, 2016
5 Lee, 2015
6 Levenson, 2017
7 For a follow-up podcast on this case, and the impact it had on the autistic man, see Quinn (2018).
8 Asperger/Autism Network, n.d.
9 Autism Society of Alabama, n.d.
10 Gargaro *et al.*, 2011
11 de Marchena, Eigsti, & Yerys, 2015
12 Genderqueer Chicago, n.d.
13 Also known as comic strip conversations (National Autistic Society, 2018).
14 Dimbort *et al.*, 2005
15 Code-switching is, linguistically and culturally, "the act of altering how you express yourself based on your audience" (McWilliams, 2018).

SHERRY

Sherry is a 28-year-old Caucasian and Jewish transgender woman who identifies as queer, bisexual, and on the asexual spectrum. Born in Arkansas, she previously lived in Vermont, where she had a farm and ran for political office. More recently, she has settled in Seattle. Self-diagnosed with autism and not interested in a formal diagnosis, Sherry is very active in the transgender and autistic communities. She uses she/her pronouns. "Sherry" is a pseudonym.

COMING OUT AS AUTISTIC

Sherry's mother, who has an undergraduate degree in psychology, noted that she was awkward in public and didn't have many friends. It was at this time that her mother broached the idea that she may have Asperger's syndrome. However, formal diagnosis wasn't pursued at the time, and she didn't revisit the possibility until she was about 23 years old, when she was friends with a person who was diagnosed with autism. Sherry found that she was better able to understand and communicate with her autistic friends than the neurotypical world, which prompted her to investigate the autistic diagnostic criteria and symptomatology, and ultimately to conclude that they fitted her. She has since communicated this to her doctors and healthcare professionals, who noted it on her medical records.

Sherry characterizes her coming out as a very gradual and positive process that has helped her to find and connect with a larger community of people with similar communication styles. The only downside has been that people who don't know her sometimes don't believe that she is autistic, owing to her relatively articulate and verbal nature and, in most cases, lack of outward autistic symptoms. She has, in fact, been accused of making it up in order to seek unnecessary accommodations at the expense of people who are "really autistic" (that is, more closely resembling an autistic stereotype or caricature).

COMING OUT AS TRANSGENDER

Sherry has very early childhood memories of wondering what it would be like to be a girl. While growing up, she primarily explored her gender identity through crossdressing, first when she was 11, then more regularly from age 14. At the time, because she lacked more nuanced language, she referred to herself as a crossdresser who hoped to "go 24/7" in the future. She began to identify as transsexual at 18 and, in her freshman year of college, to dress in feminine clothes while at school. Unfortunately, her parents were hostile to her gender identity and gave her an ultimatum to stop or move out. She did live on her own briefly but found balancing school and work to be overwhelming; she was ultimately forced to move back in with her parents and go back in the closet. Sherry didn't come out again until she was 22 and living on her own. She has been out since.

LINKS BETWEEN AUTISM AND GENDER IDENTITY

Sherry is skeptical about the suggestion that autism and gender identity might be intrinsically linked and feels that their coincidence may have more to do with the tendency of autistic people to bow to tradition or take social conventions as immutable. For instance, she notes that an autistic child might be less inclined to take a parent's assertion they are male solely because of the gender to which they were assigned at birth, as opposed to how they might identify their gender identity. Sherry feels that, generally, autistic children are more likely to explore and think deeply about their own gender identity.

FAMILY

Sherry's younger sibling is also transgender and she feels that her biological children are most likely autistic. As noted, her mother and stepfather were abusive, and punished her for her gender identity and for behaviours and symptoms related to autism. As a result, she hasn't had any contact with them in person for almost ten years, and not at all since coming out as autistic. Sherry characterizes her father, with whom she sometimes speaks on the phone, as more accepting in that he has made attempts to understand her life.

COMMUNITY AND ACTIVISM

Sherry is very involved in multiple autistic and transgender communities that intersect with various facets of her identity, particularly Judaism, political interests, and hobbies. She also participates in organizing workshops for transgender and autistic people. Sherry also recently ran for political office; though she didn't win, she did do unexpectedly well and enjoyed the opportunity to share her message with the public.

WORK

Sherry didn't disclose many negative work experiences, possibly because her work history has been limited due to disabilities unrelated to autism. She reported working in software development, specifically in the creation of healthcare software and, before leaving her graduate program, a smartphone app. She has also worked on a farm in Vermont with her chosen family and, as mentioned above, ran for political office.

HEALTHCARE

Sherry's healthcare experience has been mixed. For instance, her therapist at the time was very hostile to her coming out as transsexual. As a person who is multiply disabled, she has also been frustrated with the amount of time it takes to get a proper diagnosis and the tendency of some professionals to assign blame for various unrelated concerns to her transgender identity (e.g. "trans broken arm syndrome"). As regards accommodations and supports, Sherry often uses a cane or wheelchair and, on rare occasions, brings her cat along for emotional support.

Though she is aware that autistic people tend to face greater barriers when accessing transitional care, Sherry feels she didn't experience this as she came out as autistic after beginning transition. In addition, she shares that medical practitioners may now be more knowledgeable about the overlap between transgender identity and autism, and therefore less likely to deny them transitional care or treat their transgender identity as an inherent disorder. By contrast, when she was younger, those with mental health issues were disqualified from transgender care.

MEDIA REPRESENTATION

Sherry has seen some media representations of people who are transgender or autistic, including in video games, and is aware of actors who are transgender. However, she notes that it is often difficult to tell if a character is explicitly autistic, as this almost always seems to be portrayed through subtext. As a result, she relies largely on what she calls "head canon,"[1] which is the fandom-inspired process of interpreting a fictional text through a personal lens, and personally accepting as true elements which may be at most implicit in the source material— in Sherry's case, claiming a character with autistic traits as autistic. For example, though not explicitly characterized as such in the game, Sherry considers the character Aurene, from the MMORPG *Guild Wars 2*,[2] to be autistic, because she is a baby dragon that expresses autistic traits such as flapping her legs when happy, and not understanding social conventions.

SOCIAL RULES

Sherry describes how, as a child, she had a great deal of trouble navigating social rules and conventions and, as a result, became very comfortable questioning those that don't make sense. She characterizes herself as gender non-conforming and shares that she plays with and subverts gender role expectations, embracing some while throwing others out. This has led some people to see her as more confrontational and franker than is expected of a feminine transgender woman. In general, Sherry notes that many social norms, particularly those for women, are exceedingly indirect and exhaust her patience. Finally, she does feel that people treat her differently due to her being visibly transgender and expects that this will continue for a long time. She doesn't have the same experience with people noticing her autism, though she feels that this would help to avoid misunderstandings.

FINAL THOUGHTS

Sherry's experience of autism and transgender identity has been mixed. The barriers she has experienced have been significant, particularly with regards to her family of origin and healthcare experiences. Her multiple physical disabilities have added their own challenges. However, her connections with other transgender and autistic people, both individually and as an activist, have enabled her to weather and perhaps grow stronger from these experiences. In some ways, Sherry's experience is singular. She is, for example, the only participant to have run for political office, or lived and worked on a farm. Sherry was also one of the few participants to state that her experience of obtaining transitional healthcare has not been made more difficult by autism which, by her own assessment, may be a result of coming out as autistic after beginning transition.

Sherry's experiences are, however, also echoed in many of the other interviews. She falls, for instance, roughly in the middle of the age range of other participants interviewed (21–36 years old). As regards sexuality, Sherry is one of nine participants who explicitly expressed a queer identity (e.g. gay, lesbian, queer, bisexual, pansexual) and four who identified as asexual or greysexual. She also shares her Jewish identity with at least one other participant. As with three other participants, Sherry's autism is self-diagnosed because she hasn't had the opportunity or felt the need to pursue a formal diagnosis, which can be quite expensive and difficult to obtain. Unfortunately, her negative experience with her family of origin is also not unusual. She has been able to achieve a somewhat supportive relationship with her father, though she continues to have no contact with her mother and stepfather. However, the support and meaning Sherry has found in transgender and autistic community activism appear to act as a counterpoint to issues with her family of origin.

Sherry's mixed experience with healthcare, and hostile care providers who tend to blame unrelated health problems on transgender identity, is also reflected by other participants, as is her frustration with long and sometimes incomprehensible waiting periods. Like many others, Sherry has had healthcare professionals react with hostility to her gender identity and, on other occasions, refuse to accept that she is autistic. However, she also ultimately feels that transgender healthcare access has improved dramatically for both neurotypical and autistic people.

ENDNOTES
1   Kurchak, 2018
2   ArenaNet, 2012

TRISTAN

Tristan is a 25-year-old white, queer, transgender man, who also sometimes identifies as genderqueer. He was born in Kansas and currently lives in North Carolina. Tristan was formally diagnosed with autism in 2016. He has opted to use his real name and he/him pronouns.

COMING OUT AS AUTISTIC

It was an article in an online humour magazine that first helped Tristan to understand his relationship to autism; this article pointed out the various similarities between the *Star Trek* character Spock, and people with autism. This helped Tristan to understand why he had always related so much to a character other people criticized for "being too logical and not emotional enough." Tristan related strongly to "the idea of having an unemotional exterior [and] a very deep internal emotional landscape that [he] struggled to manage."

Tristan received a formal autism diagnosis in 2016. He pursued the diagnosis because one was required to access disability-related academic accommodations at his university. The university did not agree to cover the cost of the required neuropsychological assessment which, had Tristan not had insurance, would have been over $1,000. Fortunately, his insurance brought it down to a $20 co-pay. Tristan later found out that his mother had considered, then decided against, getting him tested for autism as a child, because she feared it would make him feel "more different than [he] already did."

Tristan's diagnostic experience was largely negative, primarily because the practice he consulted didn't handle his comorbidities well. Instead, he reports that they fixated on autism to the point of completely ignoring other issues, particularly OCD and ADHD. Tristan didn't learn that he tested as having "severe" OCD until he requested his diagnostic records, though the assessor had opined that there was a lot of overlap between this condition and autism.

Tristan was also frustrated by the way in which the assessor approached the diagnosis itself. For instance, she assumed that he had already been diagnosed with Asperger's, even though he was clear he hadn't, and focused primarily on whether he had "mechanical interests, like trains, as a child." Tristan recalls additionally that she partially based her remark that he "was obviously very high functioning" on his SAT scores.[1]

Tristan found it odd that, in his medical records, the assessor described him as both "trans-gender" and "transgender" and noted that other patients wouldn't be described as cisgender. He also felt that, though he was asked to fill out a number of self-reported forms and psychiatric inventories, the results were given inconsistent weight in the final assessment. For instance, though Tristan tested in the severe range for both ADHD and autism, he only received a diagnosis of "mild Asperger's or autism." Following this rather disastrous experience, Tristan asked to be assessed by the same practice again, primarily to revisit the possibility that he had ADHD.

COMING OUT AS TRANSGENDER

For Tristan, realizing he was transgender was a very slow process that was catalyzed, in part, by discovering the book *Female Masculinity* at a local LGBT centre when he was 18 years old.[2]

After reading it, he came to identify, at least temporarily, as butch and finally as male/male adjacent when he was around 20 years old. Tristan explains that his autism, and specifically his tendency to see things literally, was a factor in why it took him so long to come to this conclusion. He elaborates that, when he was first exploring gender identity, Tumblr wasn't yet a major community hub and most online resources referenced only male-to-female and female-to-male people. Tristan didn't identify with the latter because he imagined that it meant that one "literally changed from a girl into a guy, [and since he] never felt like a girl in the first place," he couldn't understand how this was possible for him. As a result, he concluded that he "wasn't trans, just bad at being a girl."

Tristan also had trouble with the assumption that transgender men had to be stereotypically masculine. By contrast, the men he admired were people like Gerard Way, from the band My Chemical Romance, and Dr. Frank-N-Furter, a character in the *Rocky Horror Picture Show*.[3] Tristan's tendency to think literally, and take existing examples as prescriptive, caused him to feel that it wasn't possible to be a transgender man who had a different expression of masculinity. It wasn't until identities like demiboy, genderfluid, and feminine boy proliferated on sites like Tumblr that he found ones that mirrored his own. Tristan now fluctuates between identifying as a guy, which is true most of the time, and feeling more comfortable with the term non-binary.

Tristan's transitional journey has been similarly slow and measured. He started by changing his name legally, though he didn't initially ask anyone to alter the pronouns they used for him, beyond specifying that they not call him "it." Tristan subsequently came out to his mother when she was drunk and recalls that she asked him "if [he] wanted a penis." He responded that he didn't, to which she replied "good, penises aren't that great." Tristan then came out to his father, who initially "thought that he was just trying to escape the way women are treated in society [and that] he wouldn't be having this 'gender confusion' if they hadn't let [him] play with both boys and girls toys [as] a kid." He reports, nevertheless, that his parents have largely got used to it, and that they rarely misgender him anymore. Tristan has now been on testosterone for over four years.

LINKS BETWEEN AUTISM AND GENDER IDENTITY

When asked to consider the relationship between transgender identity and autism, Tristan admitted that he hadn't actually thought that much about it. He clarified that "being trans and being autistic are both such integral parts of who I am that I don't know what causes the other." After considering it, however, Tristan concluded that he didn't think that "autism made me a boy, or that being a boy made me autistic." Regardless, autism is intertwined with his ability to envision, articulate, and act on his gender identity via transition. For instance, as an autistic person, it is difficult for Tristan to decode and navigate contradictory and inconsistent standards of masculinity, and he notes that gender is inherently confusing to him, as it is inseparable from social norms. Nevertheless, he rejects the notion that an autistic person is incapable of identifying and expressing a transgender identity, not least because of its ableist implications.

FAMILY

Tristan has a close relationship with his family, who, while struggling initially, have come to be fairly supportive of his autism and gender identity. In fact, when he informed his mother about the former, her first response was "Well, I'm not surprised." Tristan also suspects that his father and sibling are "on the spectrum." However, in discussing this with them, he learned that his sibling, who is also non-binary, is okay with this, while his father indicated that he preferred not to be "labelled." Tristan's family have been slower to accept him as transgender; while his siblings have been very supportive, his parents, though much more supportive now than initially, have had more difficulty.

COMMUNITY AND ACTIVISM

Tristan initially characterized himself as not very involved in the transgender or autistic communities. However, after exploring this topic in more depth, Tristan clarified that he is engaged in providing transgender services for his local LGBT centre and, more recently, worked to start a discussion group for autistic LGBT individuals. He also hasn't participated in any autism rights organizations. Tristan does, however, assist with a yearly transgender and autistic discussion group at the annual Philadelphia Transgender Wellness Conference.[4]

WORK

Tristan works in what he describes as "a very macho" professional kitchen environment. As an autistic person, he finds this challenging, particularly understanding unspoken directions from his manager and when his co-workers are joking. In fact, in the past, Tristan was once fired due to his failure to pick up on social cues. On other occasions, however, he has been passed over for jobs because of gender non-conformity. In fact, Tristan has found that he experiences more workplace discrimination when he is out as transgender and is treated differently as an autistic person, though he attributes the latter to co-workers unconsciously responding to his different or unusual behaviour.

HEALTHCARE

It is fortuitous for Tristan that he is presently on his father's insurance plan, and therefore able to afford good healthcare. His healthcare experience has, however, been decidedly mixed. For instance, Tristan has had difficulty finding practitioners who are both compassionate to and experienced in autistic and transgender issues. While he has recently started seeing a therapist who specializes in both, for which he feels fortunate, he was forced to go without for a few years. Prior to this, Tristan had seen a therapist who was good with transgender issues, but reluctant to accept or address his autism, instead making a point of dismissing it by saying things like "Well, if you think you have autism." This, coupled with their insistence on using person-first language (e.g. person with autism), led him to avoid talking about the issue at all. The therapist's use of, and worse insistence on, person-first language suggests that they were either unaware of, or unconcerned about, linguistic developments and preferences on this issue.[5]

Regarding denial of transgender healthcare, Tristan sees himself as lucky in that he didn't obtain a diagnosis of autism until he had started testosterone and had had "top surgery." Providers were not, as a result, able to use autism as a reason to enact greater barriers to, or outright deny, transitional care. Tristan finds that his transgender identity is more problematic than his autism when it comes to accessing healthcare. For instance, when obtaining non-transgender-related healthcare services, as for a cold, he is forced to decide what medical history to share for fear of outing himself and possibly impacting the quality of treatment he receives. As discussed, this is widely known as "trans broken arm syndrome." Similarly, many transgender people report being asked, particularly in emergency departments, inappropriate and invasive questions and even coerced to show their genitals to curious professionals.[6,7]

MEDIA REPRESENTATION

Tristan has never seen his experience as a transgender and autistic person reflected in popular media. He can, however, identify characters that represent the experience of one or the other, such as in *Orange Is the New Black*,[8] and the most recent *Power Rangers* movie.[9] Broadly speaking, however, Tristan feels that media representation is awful for both transgender and autistic people, particularly when he was younger, as evidenced by his having to identify with Spock from *Star Trek*,[10] who was literally an alien.

SOCIAL RULES

As noted, Tristan has a lot of difficulty with social rules and conventions, particularly in understanding and navigating masculinity among cisgender men. His work in a kitchen, which is a stereotypically "macho" environment, makes this more difficult and fraught. Tristan's experience of employment has also been affected by his autism and transgender identity. He relates that not understanding social norms makes it harder to understand what co-workers are trying to communicate and can't, for example, always tell if people are joking, or if he is missing nuance.

FINAL THOUGHTS

Tristan is a young, Caucasian, queer, transgender, and gender-queer man living in the southern United States. He was slow to understand himself and come out as transgender. Tristan attributes this to autism causing him to see things literally and failing to understand that gender expression could encompass something other than stereotypical or binary masculinity. The proliferation of multiple expressions of gender identity via sites like Tumblr helped him to understand this wasn't the case and he has since pursued transition in a measured and intentional manner.

Tristan's experience of transgender and autistic healthcare has, however, been mixed. For instance, while he ably navigates barriers and gatekeeping, he also has had trouble finding compassionate and experienced practitioners for either concern. Tristan has also had to hide his autism or gender identity from practitioners in order to receive unbiased healthcare, though he has never been denied transitional care for being autistic, perhaps because he didn't receive a diagnosis until after starting transition. He did, however, have a particularly frustrating experience pursuing an autism diagnosis and often finds that unrelated healthcare problems are attributed to his gender identity (e.g. "trans broken arm syndrome").

Tristan's employment experiences have been similarly mixed. For instance, he works in a very macho kitchen environment with a high expectation of non-verbal communication. This is difficult for him and he often has trouble understanding workplace expectations and whether co-workers are joking or serious. As a result, while Tristan's experience of workplace discrimination due to gender identity is overt, that related to autism is subtler, though still present.

Tristan has a close relationship with his family. His parents, though not always supportive of his gender identity, have made great strides in understanding and accepting him. Tristan also derives support from the larger transgender and autistic community and has assisted in facilitating an annual workshop for individuals who are transgender and autistic.

Autism and gender identity are, for Tristan, intertwined. He regards gender, which is inseparable from social definitions, roles, and expectations, as a particularly confusing concept for an autistic person. Nevertheless, Tristan is firm and happy in his identity as a transgender man and hopeful for future opportunities to contribute to the autism and transgender communities.

ENDNOTES

1 Smith, 2017
2 Halberstam, 1998
3 Adler, White, & Sharman, 1975
4 Philadelphia Transgender Wellness Conference, n.d.
5 Fletcher-Watson, 2016
6 Chisolm-Straker *et al.*, 2017
7 Brown, 2011
8 Tannenbaum, 2013
9 Saban *et al.*, 2017
10 Roddenberry, 1966

CONCLUSION

NOTHING ABOUT US WITHOUT US

The motto *Nothing about us without us*, or *Nihil de nobis, sine nobis* in the original Latin, originated in 16th-century Central Europe.[1] It asserts that no decisions should be made without the active participation of the group affected by them and includes their capacity to give and revoke consent. The motto has been central to disability,[2] HIV,[3] and transgender[4] activism and is one of the central tenets of autism activism, particularly where social policy and research are concerned. It is also the central idea around which this book is formed, and frames the exploration of the interviews that takes place in this chapter.

ANSWERS TO QUESTIONS ASKED
Coming out as autistic

Our participants had many different experiences of diagnosis with regards to autism. In general, these can be summarized as receiving a diagnosis as a child, receiving a diagnosis as an adult, and being self-diagnosed. There is, however, some fluidity between these last two categories. Alex, Isabella, Nami, and Moose were diagnosed as children. Alex found this to be largely positive, though they were frustrated that they weren't told about their diagnosis until several years afterwards. Nevertheless, this information and their parents' support greatly helped them to find their place in the larger autistic community.

Isabella, Nami, and Moose also found their place in the autistic community, although their paths there were quite different, as were their experiences of family support. All three, however, worried that, as Asians, their autism might "shame" their families and lead to rejection. Isabella's immediate and extended family were able to accept this information after other family members were diagnosed with autism. Nami and Moose's families, however, had more difficulty. This may, in part, explain why Nami describes herself as "broken" and Moose justifies his mother's abusive behaviour as being rationalized by the aforementioned stigma.

Reynard and Tristan were formally diagnosed with autism as adults after exploring the subject and receiving neuroeducational assessments at university. Reynard described this as a very positive process that helped them understand that their manner of interacting with the world was valid. In contrast, Tristan had a very negative experience, finding the process stigmatizing and the assessors overly fixated on autism to the neglect of other concerns. Interestingly, Reynard and Tristan both initially sought a diagnosis for ADHD. Reynard was subsequently surprised to be diagnosed with autism instead. Tristan, however, was frustrated that the assessor focused on autism to the seeming exclusion of ADHD.

Grace, James, and Sherry are self-diagnosed with autism, as was Nathan initially. Grace and Sherry both relayed that their parents noticed they were "different" as children but rejected obtaining a diagnosis. James first considered autism shortly before discovering his gender identity. Nathan, for his part, explored the subject after noticing similarities between himself and autistic characters on television. His initial self-diagnosis was affirmed by his employer, who is a psychologist, before being confirmed by his own psychologist. Similarly, Sherry has informed her healthcare practitioners that she is autistic and had it noted on her medical records.

Several participants related that either they or their parents avoided an autism diagnosis out of concern that it would contribute to the stigmatization they faced on an everyday basis. Some praised this strategy as helping them to succeed in the neurotypical world by "feigning normality when necessary." It may also, in the long run, have contributed to internalized ableism, as well as avoidance and even bullying of other autistic people. Grace, for instance, talked about how recognizing "similar thought processes and behaviours in others...can [cause her to] become vicariously anxious." This might not have been the case if she was allowed to embrace herself as autistic at a young age, without fear of social exclusion or harassment.

In fact, many participants expressed relief at finding out that they weren't alone and that their problems with, for instance, making friends and eye contact were attributable to autism rather than simply being "bad." This knowledge allowed them to connect with the larger autistic community and understand that their way of interacting with the world is valid. Nevertheless, there was wide agreement that some autism interventions, such as ABA, are ineffectual and even harmful.[5] Participants argued that this is the case because they rely on forcing autistic children to hide or mask their autism and often use dehumanizing methods to do so.

In fact, masking or camouflaging autistic traits can limit the availability of support by making it more difficult to be recognized as autistic,[6] particularly for those who are assigned female at birth.[7] Regardless of assigned sex at birth, many of our participants expressed frustration with being told that they couldn't be autistic because they were "too verbal" or "made eye contact." Sherry, for instance, has been accused of faking autism in order to access accommodations. Alex had to purposefully discard the masking strategies taught to them in order to accept themselves and integrate into the autism community.

COMING OUT AS TRANSGENDER

There was no unified version of the transgender coming-out narrative. Instead, participants had a wide variety of different experiences that also shared a number of similarities. For instance, most recalled having uncertainty around or questioning their gender identity at a very young age. None, however, received active support from their parents to explore this subject and, as a result, suppressed these feelings due to confusion, shame, and fear of both parents and peers.

Of course, their transgender identities never went away and usually re-emerged during their late teens or early twenties. Alex, Grace, and Tristan credit the website Tumblr with enabling them to explore the diversity of gender expression and identity both within and outside the binary (e.g. male and female). Media also played a big role, with Alex, Grace, James, and Tristan identifying a specific book, video game, documentary, or television show in helping to catalyze their understanding of themselves as transgender.

Most participants indicated that their transgender friends were central to them exploring their own gender identity. Meeting another transgender person helped Alex, Grace, and Reynard to realize that their transgender identity did not have to mirror the stereotypes portrayed on television. Much as with autism, it also prompted Grace and Isabella to re-examine the ways in which they had engaged in transphobia, out of fear of being identified as transgender. Almost all participants continue to find support and solidarity in the transgender community.

Most participants came out to the larger world in stages. Several informed friends and supportive family members first. Their parents' reactions ranged from acceptance, to slow acceptance, and outright rejection and disownment. Most fell in the middle, with initial concerns, and difficulty adapting to pronoun and name changes. Isabella, Moose, Nami, and Sherry, meanwhile, experienced different degrees of total rejection. In no case, however, did this rejection stop them from pursuing transition. In fact, all participants have undertaken some form of transition, whether name and pronoun changes, or hormonal and surgical interventions. And almost all emphasized a desire to contemplate transitional goals carefully and take transition slowly.

Some participants also indicated that their sexuality had shifted since transitioning. James, Reynard, and Tristan, for instance, identified as a lesbian because they assumed that their masculinity coupled with a female gender assignment mandated it. While identifying as bisexual/pansexual prior to transition, Grace found herself far more attracted to women and femininity than previously. James characterized this period of his life as "almost asexual" and has since come to identify as gay.

LINKS BETWEEN AUTISM AND GENDER IDENTITY

Participants were divided as to whether autism and gender identity are inherently linked. That is to say, whether autism causes an individual to be transgender or vice versa. Alex, for instance, felt strongly that, at least in their case, both are linked. Grace, James, and Nami were less certain, and felt that it could be an unrelated correlation. Isabella and Moose, for their part, felt strongly that autism and gender identity weren't related. Nathan, Reynard, Sherry, and Tristan, however, allowed for the possibility while remaining skeptical. This last group also concluded that it ultimately didn't matter, except where access to transitional care was jeopardized, or autism made it more difficult to understand concepts like gender.

Several participants commented on why autism and transgender identity might appear to be connected. They hypothesized that autistic people tend to be non-conforming generally, have difficulty picking up unspoken norms, and are inclined to explore and question social rules and expectations. Alex noted that gender is a flimsy social construct that can often seem nonsensical to people on the autism spectrum. As a result, while some transgender autistic individuals are strongly aware of an internal gender, their desire to conform to gendered social expectations may be limited. Nami suggested that there may only appear to be a link between autism and transgender identity because autistic people are less able to mimic cisgender behaviours or otherwise hide their transgender identity.

Most nevertheless felt that their experience of exploring their gender identity was affected by autism. Alex indicated that, as a child, they accepted the gender bestowed on them as inevitable, if distasteful, until they became aware of language to describe their experiences and others like them. James explained that he tends to gravitate towards rigid notions of transition because autism makes it difficult for him to accept uncertainty. Moose indicated that, though he is uncertain if it's related to feeling more comfortable in his environment, his autistic symptoms (e.g. stimming, rocking) did become more pronounced after starting testosterone. Moose and Tristan both shared that they have trouble understanding and navigating often contradictory and inconsistent standards of masculinity. All participants, however, are happy with their current gender identity and expression.

FAMILY

The individuals interviewed for this book had a variety of different experiences with their families of origin, ranging from acceptance and support, to outright rejection. With regards to autism, Grace hasn't really broached the subject with her parents, while Alex and Tristan's have been very supportive. Isabella's family, despite initially having some difficulty, came to be supportive after several of her cousins received a similar diagnosis. Nathan's parents are supportive, though his father struggles to accommodate his desire for minimal physical contact. Conversely, James's family have dismissed the idea of him having autism, and Moose, Nami, and Sherry's parents rejected and/or punished them for it. Reynard, for their part, found support only from their brother and father's family. Interestingly, all but three knew or suspected that other members of their family were on the autism spectrum.

No participant described their family as being universally supportive with regards to transgender identity. Alex, for instance, described their parents as initially struggling to understand their non-binary gender identity and some members of their extended family as negative about this aspect of their identity. Over time, however, they have come to experience a remarkable level of support from their immediate and extended family. Alternatively, Isabella has been supported by her brothers, but not her parents, who characterize her transgender identity as a deviance. Moose, Nami, and Sherry's parents felt similar and reacted by issuing ultimatums or cutting off contact. For James, contrary to their reaction to his disclosure of autism, all extended family members except one have been very supportive. Grace, Nathan, and Tristan found that their parents needed some time to come to terms with and process the information, but all consider their parents very supportive now. Finally, as with autism, Reynard's brother and father's family are immensely supportive.

Nami attributed her family's lack of support to the social expectations placed on children in East Asian culture. In fact, Nami, as well as Isabella and Moose, shared their East Asian background and experience of parental rejection due to being transgender and/or autistic. Nathan and Reynard, however, described their Black/African-American relatives as ultimately being unconditionally supportive, though they also identified the ways in which these relatives consider their autistic traits to be culturally out of sync. In Reynard's case, some relatives blame this on their being partially white.

COMMUNITY AND ACTIVISM

Community was an essential component of every individual's life and, for most, activism was as well. In fact, both Moose and Reynard moved to different cities to be closer to the transgender and/or autistic communities. Participants credit these groups with learning to accept themselves, and meeting others like them, finding friends, and as a source of solidarity and help. In Isabella and Moose's case, however, work schedules and income have made participation in these communities more difficult. For Moose specifically, racist police checkpoints (e.g. "stop and frisks") have been a particular barrier to accessing LGBTQ and autism supports. Alex also noted that they had to unlearn the "normalizing" behaviours forced on them by ABA, in order to fully participate in the autism community.

Regarding individual contributions, Alex co-founded a group for autistic people in Ontario,[8] and Reynard has been instrumental in reviving and diversifying a group for transgender individuals. Nathan manages an academic transgender health lab,[9] helps to organize an annual conference[10] for transgender youth and their parents, and has presented research originating from the aforementioned lab at international academic conferences.[11,12] Isabella volunteered with LGBT youth providing peer counselling and services for homelessness and suicide prevention. Nami mentored autistic people and worked in the LGBTQ community as a sexual health educator, advocate, and support person for refugees. Moose was the subject of media coverage for furthering transgender inclusivity in his role on the young adult leadership of his church. Sherry ran for political office, and Tristan has helped to facilitate an annual workshop for transgender and autistic people. In addition, Judaism and the Jewish community have been central to Alex and Sherry's lives.

HEALTHCARE

Participants reported a number of physical, neurological, and mental disabilities in addition to autism. For instance, Grace, Nathan, and Tristan have OCD, while Alex, Isabella, Reynard, and Tristan have ADHD. Social or generalized anxiety disorder has been an issue for Alex, Grace, Nathan, and Reynard. Finally, Alex and Isabella both have a learning disability. Some participants also contend with physical disabilities like fibromyalgia, chronic fatigue syndrome, and migraines.

Participants' experiences navigating healthcare with regards to autism were mixed. Alex had largely positive experiences with early autism diagnosis and treatment. Their experience with their dentist and as the recipient of physical restraints during school was, however, decidedly more negative. Similarly, Isabella was happy with the autism healthcare she received, but upset that her placement in a special education classroom provided her with a substandard education. Nami was traumatized by the haphazard and dangerous way in which her parents modified her physical therapy. Moose's experience of early autism diagnosis was traumatic, primarily because his parents refused to accept it. Others, like James, Nathan, and Tristan, encountered difficulties in having healthcare professionals take them seriously with regards to their autism, or provide help with this. Similarly, both Alex and Tristan struggled with being misdiagnosed in neuropsychiatric assessments.

Transitional healthcare experiences were also mixed. Alex, for instance, struggles with trying to separate the healthcare interventions they genuinely want, from what is expected of them as a non-binary person. They, as well as Reynard, Sherry, and Tristan, also worry about or have experienced the phenomenon of healthcare practitioners blaming unrelated problems on their transgender status. Finally, Moose and Reynard were careful to hide their autism after being denied transitional care due to it, while Sherry and Tristan didn't experience this issue as they came out as autistic after starting transitioning.

Several participants struggled to find a competent provider of autism and/or transgender healthcare. Grace, for instance, chose to take the initiative of educating her doctor in the provision of transgender healthcare rather than wait for a rare spot at a clinic dedicated to transgender healthcare. Her doctor has been willing to do so, despite also being frustratingly rigid in interpreting and applying the relevant medical guidelines.[13,14] James, likewise, had difficulty finding a GP who was both competent to provide transgender healthcare and willing to. Indeed, his GP initially refused to refer him to a specialist transgender health service, then to continue the treatment prescribed by this service. Nathan and Tristan, for their part, have had difficulty finding therapists who are knowledgeable about dealing with autism.

MEDIA REPRESENTATION

Participants were able to identify several examples of popular media with autistic characters. This consisted of characters in TV shows that are explicitly autistic, like *The Good Doctor*,[15] *Atypical*,[16] *Parenthood*,[17] and *Degrassi*,[18] and those coded autistic, such as Sheldon in *The Big Bang Theory*.[19] Other media mentioned included biopics and documentaries, such as *Temple Grandin*,[20] and movies like *Mozart and the Whale*,[21] *Power Rangers*,[22] and *Marathon*.[23] Regarding popular media with transgender characters, *Degrassi* was again mentioned, as well as *Orange Is the New Black*,[24] *Boy Meets Girl*,[25] and *Steven Universe*.[26] The documentaries *The Boy Who Was Born a Girl*[27] and *Genderquake*[28] were also noted.

Most participants felt that representation for transgender and autistic issues alone was poor and for transgender/autistic ones almost non-existent. Regarding the former, the little that existed was often characterized as "horrific, simplified, and/or sensationalist" (Grace) and tended to focus on the experiences of people who are straight and Caucasian, while ignoring those who are, for instance, people of colour, intersex, asexual, and/or non-binary. This is particularly problematic since, as Alex noted, the general public tends to take these representations as universal and prescriptive (e.g. *Rain Man*[29]).

As a result, the individuals interviewed tended to be drawn to less mainstream outlets such as indie comic books, podcasts, and user-created content like fanart and fanfiction as more realistically depicting their lives and experiences. In fact, several participated in the creation of the latter and often made use of head canon to do so. Others sought to explore their autism and gender identities through other media, like the MMORPGs *Guild Wars 2*,[30] *World of Warcraft*,[31] *Clone Wars Adventures*,[32] and *Star Wars: The Old Republic*;[33] the *My Little Pony*[34] fandom; or books like *Dreadnought*,[35] *Female Masculinity*,[36] and *Asperger's Huh?*[37] Tumblr blogs and Facebook groups were also popular areas for exploration.

SOCIAL RULES

Unsurprisingly, most participants struggled to understand and navigate social rules and expectations, especially those related to gender roles. Alex, for instance, noted that non-binary people are expected to perform their gender in a particular way that doesn't align with their own non-binary identity.[38] Others, like Grace, had trouble separating inability (or more frankly, disinterest) in performing stereotypical masculinity from an underlying transgender identity. Alternatively, several noted that their relative imperviousness to social expectations was a net positive, in that it protected them from (and allowed them to subvert) expectations related to relatively arbitrary gender roles.

Participants also experienced new problems after coming out as transgender and transitioning. James and Tristan, for instance, have difficulty understanding unspoken rules regarding masculinity, dating, and male friendships. James expressed frustration with the fact that he receives affirmation for demonstrating the same stereotypically masculine behaviours he used to be punished for. Isabella and Nami, as transfeminine individuals, were concerned about anticipating and navigating the potential for transmisogynistic violence, which Isabella regarded as particularly tied to whiteness.

Moose's experience, however, was unique, as he is in the position of decoding and disentangling gendered social expectations of men in Japan, where he was born and raised, and the US, where he now lives. Nathan and Reynard also remarked on tensions between social expectations in the Black community and their own experience of autism. Nathan noted, for instance, that the Black community's emphasis on respect tends to lead them to view autistic behaviour as defiance. Reynard, for their part, shared that the Black community prizes directness and, as a result, tends to see them as reserved, while the white community does the opposite.

Finally, both James and Reynard identified a connection between their impaired ability to pick up social cues and expectations with their tendency to walk into dangerous situations. In James's case, this has involved not noticing that he is receiving homophobic street abuse until his partner tells him. Reynard, on the other hand, characterizes themselves as very prone to sexual assault, because people incorrectly infer consent from their actions (or inaction) and they sometimes fail to notice when situations are becoming sexual.

ANSWERS TO QUESTIONS NOT ASKED
People of colour

Participants were widely and intentionally diverse. Five are white (two Jewish), three Asian, and two Black/African American. Of the latter five, three also identify as bi/multiracial. Despite this, no specific interview question addressed their experiences of autism in relation to racial or ethnic identity. The topic nevertheless arose frequently and spontaneously. We were, as a result, able to explore how people of colour navigate autism and transgender identity and the ways in which their racial and ethnic identities impact their access to resources and even safety.

Nathan noted that Black people prize the virtue of cleanliness due to historical and contemporary experiences of racism. He explained that, in his experience, this has led the community to interpret some OCD symptoms as inherently positive. Both Nathan and Reynard spoke about how Black communities interpret aspects of their autism as defiance or "weirdness." In fact, some research shows that Black parents report fewer concerns about autism or autistic symptoms like repetitive behaviour.[39] Other reports detail the culturally specific responses of parents to autism and related behaviours[40,41] and note that they may lead Black children to be diagnosed later than white children.[42]

Reynard observed that authorities such as parents, teachers, and police have tended to view their autistic traits as acts of defiance because they are Black. This has led to several tense and even dangerous situations that caused them to fear for their safety. Reynard recalled, for instance, a case in which the (Black) behavioural therapist of an autistic man was shot because police mistook the (Puerto Rican) autistic man's toy truck for a firearm.[43,44] They further pointed out that police interaction tools designed for these situations don't consider that Black and masculine people may not be safe to retrieve them from their pockets when they are around police.[45]

Moose, for his part, wasn't able to access autism or LGBTQ supports in New Orleans due to being continuously "stopped and frisked" when attempting to enter the neighbourhoods in which they were located. Interestingly, this occurred in both Black and white neighbourhoods because, as an Asian man, he didn't fit the police's conception of who should be there. In fact, a great deal has been written about law enforcement discrimination, and the impact of stop and frisk policies on queer and transgender people of colour.[46,47]

Isabella, Moose, and Reynard all reported on the overall whiteness of the autism and transgender communities. Reynard noted that this was a characteristic of the transgender group they facilitate, and that it had to be discussed openly and honestly to correct it. This may speak to differences in ethnic and racial cultural communication styles.[48] For Reynard, the Black community expects direct communication, while the white community prefers it to be indirect, especially when the issue is contentious. This is consistent with research on the subject.[49] It may therefore be useful to approach autism as a unique culture that, generally speaking, prioritizes direct verbal communication; of course, autistic traits differ across cultures.[50]

Finally, our Asian participants noted that there were unique cultural expectations attached to their behaviour in relation to gender identity and autism. Isabella, Moose, and Nami had all been disowned or otherwise experienced family sanction for expressing gender variant behaviour and/or being autistic. The Substance Abuse and Mental Health Services Administration describes a similar example in which a Japanese man in treatment was encouraged to follow their standard practice of informing his family.[51] Unfortunately, the family's immediate response was to disown him for shaming them. Moose also described his experience of the tension between cultural expectations of men and masculinity in Japan and the United States.

WORK

Although we didn't specifically ask about employment, in all but one case participants volunteered this information during interviews. All currently or previously worked in some capacity and currently earn between $0 and $67,498 USD/year (average $18,218.19). Grace, James, Nathan, and Tristan work professionally as, respectively, an employee of the Federal Government of Canada, a research assistant on an international project, the manager of an academic laboratory, and in a professional kitchen. Alex volunteers with their college's student access centre and works seasonally as a camp counsellor. Nami works periodically in event planning and management, and Moose works both part time in a gay bar and full time in an administrative job. Sherry previously worked in software development, on the creation of a smartphone app, and on a farm. Isabella didn't identify the kind of work she does but indicated that she is working long shifts in order to save up for an apartment and towards future job goals.

The work history and experience of many participants was impacted by their autism. Alex, for instance, hopes to work as a social worker with other autistic people. Grace, for her part, credits her autism with both leading her to be successful in her current job and creating difficulties in the past, particularly around finding a post-degree internship. However, Isabella worries that she will have trouble finding work if employers know she is autistic. James, Moose, and Tristan feel that their workplaces are, at least in part, less accommodating of autism than gender identity. For instance, they have received cautions and/or been passed over for positions, due to their difficulties with identifying social nuances and instructions in the workplace. Nami, however, is very limited in her ability to work consistently, multitask, or manage social interactions and, as a result, isn't able to manage a nine-to-five job.

SEX

Though we asked about sexual orientation, we did not ask about participants' experiences of sex and sexuality. The topic was, nevertheless, frequently brought up. Alex and Reynard note that the autistic community may be uniquely vulnerable to sexual assault, due to a combination of different sensory and communication needs and a lack of comprehensive and developmentally appropriate sexual education. Alex worried that this might metastasize into misogynistic attacks like the Toronto van attack.[52]

Alex and Reynard also shared their experiences of abuse in the contexts of relationships and dating. For Alex, this led to becoming entangled in emotionally abusive and manipulative relationship dynamics. They felt that the ABA-style therapy they participated in primed them for this by emphasizing compliance over their own sensory needs. Reynard, for their part, explained that their lack of awareness of non-verbal communication leads them to miss or misinterpret other people's sexual intents and results in being frequently sexually assaulted. In a similar way to Alex, they feel that their tendency to go along with what is suggested may contribute to these situations. As a result, they prefer "high protocol" situations, like BDSM, where the rules are made clear ahead of time.

In fact, there is quite a bit of emerging evidence documenting the experience of sexual assault among, and sometimes by,[53] autistic people. Taught compliance,[54] the tendency to miss or misinterpret contextual cues,[55] and a lack of population-specific sexual education[56] are cited as risk factors. The National Sexual Violence Resource Center has created a resource to help sexual assault advocates address this issue.[57] Unfortunately, a great deal of this research approaches the issue from the perspective of parents and caregivers who seek to address "challenging" and sometimes "deviant" behaviours. Few resources exist by and for autistic people, with some notable exceptions. [58, 59]

FINAL THOUGHTS

We have discussed the varied experiences of people who are both transgender and autistic. While ten interviews cannot represent everyone, we are clearly a diverse and varied group, with unique concerns, as well as hopes, dreams, and goals. Still, there are areas that we wish we would have addressed more directly and substantially.

For instance, while we did not directly ask about religion, it was spontaneously addressed by two participants. These participants found Judaism to be a very meaningful part of their lives and their experiences of transgender identity and autism. Alex, for example, is heavily involved in their local Jewish community and has found a lot of meaning from traditional Jewish observations on gender. Sherry also spoke unprompted about her experience as a person who is transgender, autistic, and an observant Jew. It seems apparent that this conversation would have been more fulsome, with more people commenting on their experiences with religion, had we specifically mentioned this subject.

Nevertheless, we hope that other transgender and autistic people will see themselves and their experiences reflected in this book, especially the interviews that form its core. It is they who motivated and made this work possible. We also hope that healthcare practitioners will take this information to heart and consider the ways in which their decisions may harm us, both directly and indirectly. We wish nothing more than to be treated as human beings worthy of the same respect and dignity as those who are neurotypical.

ENDNOTES

1   Kumitz, 2016
2   Charlton, 2000
3   Pacific AIDS Network, n.d.
4   Asia Pacific Transgender Network, 2017
5   Devita-Raeburn & Spectrum, 2016
6   Russo, 2018
7   Bargiela, Steward, & Mandy, 2016
8   Autistics For Autistics, n.d.
9   Keo-Meier, n.d.
10 Gender Infinity Conference, n.d.
11 Philadelphia Transgender Wellness Conference, n.d.
12 World Professional Association for Transgender Health, n.d.
13 World Professional Association for Transgender Health, n.d.
14 Coleman *et al.*, 2012
15 Shore & DePaul, 2017
16 Gordon, 2017
17 Howard *et al.*, 2010
18 Schuyler, Stohn, & Yorke, 2002
19 Cendrowski, 2007
20 Ferguson *et al.*, 2010
21 Dimbort *et al.*, 2005
22 Saban *et al.*, 2017
23 Myeong-hong, Seung-yeop, & Chang-hwan, 2005
24 Tannenbaum, 2013
25 Kerrigan *et al.*, 2015
26 Sugar, 2013
27 Channel 4, 2009
28 Channel 4, n.d.
29 Johnson & Levinson, 1988
30 ArenaNet, 2012
31 Blizzard Entertainment, 2004
32 Daybreak Game Company, 2010
33 BioWare Austin, 2011
34 Thiessen *et al.*, 2010

35 Daniel, 2017
36 Halberstam, 1998
37 Schnurr, 1999
38 Williams, 2019
39 Donohue *et al.*, 2019
40 Bauer, Winegar, & Waxman, 2016
41 Mann, 2013
42 Gourdine, Baffour, & Teasley, 2011
43 Levenson, 2017
44 For a follow-up podcast on this case, and the impact it had on the autistic man, see Quinn (2018).
45 Asperger/Autism Network, n.d.
46 The Williams Institute, 2015
47 Morgan, 2013
48 Substance Abuse and Mental Health Services Administration, 2014
49 Asante & Davis, 1985
50 Carruthers *et al.*, 2018
51 Substance Abuse and Mental Health Services Administration, 2014, p.1
52 Monsebraaten, 2018
53 Moyer, 2019
54 Gammicchia & Johnson, 2014
55 Weiss & Fardella, 2018
56 Sevlever, Roth, & Gillis, 2013
57 National Sexual Violence Resource Center, 2018
58 Newport & Newport, 2002
59 Ashkenazy & Yergeau, 2013

FURTHER READING AND RESOURCES

The following pages list further reading and resources that expand on what is discussed in this book. Several are mentioned throughout by the individuals we interviewed and we felt that, because they are particularly apt, we should draw attention to them here. Others are discussed here for the first time. All are an excellent place to start your further reading on the topic of transgender people who are also autistic.

GROUPS

Academic Autistic Spectrum Partnership in Research and Education (AASPIRE)

http://aaspire.org

An academic partnership with autistic individuals to create and co-author research on autism. The website contains a wealth of materials and resources, both resulting from this partnership and not. In particular, check out the toolkit on primary healthcare resources for autistic adults at https://autismandhealth.org.[1]

Association for Autistic Community

http://autisticcommunity.org

An organization that supports autistic folks to grow and learn from each other. It also offers a yearly multi-day conference called Autspace.

Autism Acceptance Project

https://the-art-of-autism.com

An organization that supports and organizes exhibits of art by autistic individuals.

Autism National Committee (AUTCOM)

www.autcom.org

Founded in 1990, AUTCOM advocates for autistic civil rights and puts on an annual conference.

Autism Women & Nonbinary Network

http://autismwomensnetwork.org

An organization by and for autistic women, girls, and non-binary folks.

Autistic Self Advocacy Network (ASAN)

https://autisticadvocacy.org

ASAN advocates throughout the US for autistic rights and lobbies against aversives (e.g. shocks), restraints, and seclusion in autism treatment and education, and, in general, the idea of curing autism. It has successfully lobbied against campaigns that portray autism negatively (e.g. Autism Speaks, PETA) and runs the Autism Campus Inclusion Summer Institute, which is a week-long training for autistic college students. The latter resulted in a resource for autistic college students, available at http://navigatingcollege.org.[2] It also developed a resource on relationships and sexuality, available at http://autismnow.org/wp-content/uploads/2013/02/Relationships-and-Sexuality-Tool.pdf.[3]

Autscape

www.autscape.org

Annual UK conference by and for autistics.

MEDIA

Boy Meets Girl[4]

> A UK sitcom about transgender characters, recommended by James. Stars a transgender woman, as a transgender woman, in one of the lead roles.

Parenthood[5]

> A US television show that features a character with Asperger's (Max), which Nathan found particularly helpful. There is also a fascinating academic article[6] on the value of this character to the autism community, given the tendency to focus on autism through the lens of his parents and the larger community, rather than his own experience.

Steven Universe[7]

> An animated US television show, recommended by Alex, which features several non-binary and queer characters in prominent roles. The creator, Rebecca Sugar, also recently came out as non-binary.

The Boy Who Was Born a Girl[8]

> UK documentary, recommended by James, about a 16-year-old transgender boy in the process of transitioning.

NEWS ARTICLES AND EDITORIALS

Autism Advocacy and Research Misses the Mark if Autistic People are Left Out[9]

> https://theconversation.com/autism-advocacy-and-research-misses-the-mark-if-autistic-people-are-left-out-94404

> Article in *The Conversation* that discusses the importance of autistic people being included in campaigns and research on the subject of autism. It investigates the history of autism-led campaigns and what is gained by designing research that focuses on autistic people as co-researchers.

Autistic and Queer: Coming Out on the Spectrum[10]

> www.afterellen.com/people/424935-autistic-queer-coming-spectrum

> Article in *AfterEllen* that discusses people who are both queer and autistic. It explores the issues unique to this population in terms of dating, sex, socializing, and coming out.

Autistic New Yorkers Share Their Stim-Toy Stories with "Aftereffect"[11]

> www.npr.org/sections/health-shots/2018/07/07/625756385/autistic-new-yorkers-share-their-stim-toy-stories-with-aftereffect

> Article in *NPR* that interviews several autistic people about the self-stim toys they use. It is a response to the podcast *Aftereffect*, which discussed a case in which an autistic man's stim toy (a toy truck) was mistaken for a firearm, resulting in his personal assistant being shot. The article also presents short profiles of several autistic people.

Behind the Spotlights of Transgender China[12]

> www.whatsonweibo.com/behind-the-spotlights-of-transgender-china

> Article in *What's on Weibo* that discusses the increasing visibility of transgender people in China, particularly on the social media site Weibo, and via transgender celebrities. It explores their many positive experiences as well as more challenging issues, like legal recognition of gender and cost of sex reassignment surgery.

Face Blind[13]

> www.wired.com/2006/11/blind

> Article in *Wired* that discusses the condition face blindness, or prosopagnosia, which denotes an inability to recognize faces, and is common among those with autism.

Gender Identity in Halakhic Discourse[14]

> https://jwa.org/encyclopedia/article/gender-identity-in-halakhic-discourse

> Article in *Jewish Women's Archive* about multiple gender identities in Judaism.

Georgia's Separate and Unequal Special-Education System[15]

www.newyorker.com/magazine/2018/10/01/georgias-separate-and-unequal-special-education-system

Article in *The New Yorker* about children being warehoused and receiving substandard education in special education schools throughout Georgia, US. It follows the story of a young Black family with an autistic child.

How Our Society Harms Trans People Who Are Also Autistic[16]

https://medium.com/the-establishment/how-our-society-harms-trans-people-with-autism-9766edc6553d

Article in *The Establishment* that discusses the unique barriers faced by transgender people who are also autistic. It focuses on the tendency of transitional healthcare professionals to subject autistic people to longer waiting times and more stringent gatekeeping, and to attribute transgender identity to autism.

How Trans Players Find Support from the Gaming Community[17]

www.vice.com/en_ca/article/8gegvx/how-trans-players-find-support-from-the-gaming-community-58477ff7b003780236751598

Article in *Vice* that explores communities formed by transgender people who participate in gaming, including video and board games, and their use of these mediums to explore their own gender/s.

Imaging a Fuller Spectrum of Autism on TV[18]

https://psmag.com/social-justice/autistic-license

Article in *Pacific Standard* that discusses the importance of claiming autistic-coded characters as autistic (or head canon) to autistic individuals. It explores how autistic people use and interact with popular culture to create representations of themselves where they may not explicitly exist.

Is the Most Common Therapy for Autism Cruel?[19]

www.theatlantic.com/health/archive/2016/08/aba-autism-controversy/495272

Article in *The Atlantic* that explores the potential cruelty of applied behavioural therapy, which is the most common treatment for autism. It discusses its basis in attempts to "make people with autism 'normal'" and presents the perspectives of autism rights advocates, who strongly condemn the practice.

"It's Torture": Critics Step Up Bid to Stop School Using Electric Shocks on Children[20]

www.theguardian.com/us-news/2018/nov/16/judge-rotenberg-center-massachusetts-electric-shocks

Article in *The Guardian* that discusses the use of electric shock "aversives" at the Judge Rotenberg Center, which is a school for special needs children in Massachusetts. It also explores the campaign against this practice, led by a coalition of disability groups, including the National Autism Association.

Low Academic Expectations and Poor Support for Special Education Students are "Hurting their Future"[21]

https://hechingerreport.org/low-academic-expectations-poor-support-special-education-students-hurting-future

Article in *The Hechinger Report* that discusses the failure to provide adequate education to students in special education classrooms. It doesn't deal with autism specifically, but instead explores the effect of low academic expectations for all students with disabilities.

Meet the People Being Left Out of Mainstream Conversations About Autism[22]

www.complex.com/life/2016/04/autism-women-poc

Article in *Complex* that interviews and discusses people who are both transgender and autistic. It explores the ways in which participants defy expectations of people with autism.

Take the Autism Test[23]

www.wired.com/2001/12/aqtest

An online copy of Dr. Baron-Cohen's Autism Quotient test, which measures autism in adults, as presented in *Wired*. It can be filled in and scored on the website.

The Costs of Camouflaging Autism[24]

www.spectrumnews.org/features/deep-dive/costs-camouflaging-autism

Article in *Spectrum News* that discusses the tendency among some autistic girls and women to hide or camouflage their autism, and the ways in which this is achieved. It explores how this can result in women receiving a diagnosis later in life and that, while this behaviour can result in greater social and career advancement, it can also come at the cost of greater anxiety and isolation.

The Dangers of Trans Broken Arm Syndrome[25]

www.pinknews.co.uk/2015/07/09/feature-the-dangers-of-trans-broken-arm-syndrome

Article in *PinkNews* that discusses the phenomenon of "trans broken arm syndrome," in which healthcare practitioners blame unrelated healthcare issues on one's transgender status, and fail to treat, or insufficiently treat, the presenting issue.

The Invisibility of Black Autism[26]

https://undark.org/article/invisibility-black-autism/?fbclid=IwAR05Vo0aynvaZozZRfriXxD5k19u41dPblGtcCUWskMYBgHbo9L-BoqRMnU

Article in *Undark* about the tendency to misdiagnose autistic Black children due to institutional bias and racism.

When It Comes to Health Care, Transphobia Persists[27]

> www.theglobeandmail.com/opinion/article-when-it-comes-to-health-care-transphobia-persists

> Article in *The Globe and Mail* that discusses the extreme discrimination faced by some transgender people when seeking emergency healthcare and the tendency for healthcare professionals to fixate on the individual's transgender status, over other, more pressing issues. It follows the experience of a transgender woman in an Ontario emergency room.

BLOG POSTS

Anarchism: In the Conversations of Neurodiversity[28]

> https://maxxcrow.wordpress.com/2017/12/07/anarchism-in-the-conversations-of-neurodiversity

> Blog post that explores anarchism as a response to the societal mistreatment of neurodiverse and, more specifically, autistic individuals.

Being Nonbinary Has Nothing to Do With Looking Nonbinary[29]

> https://medium.com/@transphilosophr/being-nonbinary-has-nothing-to-do-with-looking-nonbinary-bef864483a43

> Blog post about the expectations of non-binary to present in an androgynous manner regardless of their own personal preferences.

Exploring Non-Binary Identity Theory in the Age of the Internet or Why Tumblr Might be Right About Something for Once[30]

> www.oxbowschool.org/assets/gallery/os36-final-projects/docs/sidney-h-os36paper.pdf

> Article about the ways that young queer individuals use Tumblr to explore non-binary gender identities and how this site exists as a unique place in which to do so.

Fuck You and Your Fucking Thesis: Why I Will Not Participate in Trans Studies[31]

https://tagonist.livejournal.com/199563.html#/199563.html

Blog post about the intrusiveness of research requests focused on transgender individuals and communities.

How Cultural Differences Affect Autism Diagnoses[32]

https://blogs.scientificamerican.com/guest-blog/how-cultural-differences-affect-autism-diagnoses

Blog post for *Scientific American* that explores the reliance on socially construed diagnostic criteria for an autism diagnosis. It points out that these criteria presume symptoms that are considered negative in a western context but may be normal or desirable in other contexts. This may similarly be true for groups within the western world.

It Doesn't Have to be This Hard[33]

https://tragicgenderstory.com/2017/05/11/it-doesnt-have-to-be-this-hard

Blog post from Tristan about his experiences navigating the process of autism diagnosis.

Neurowonderful[34]

www.youtube.com/channel/UC9Bk0GbW8xgvTgQlheNG5uw

YouTube channel with videos exploring the author's experience as a transgender and autistic person.

Social Stories and Comic Strip Conversations[35]

www.autism.org.uk/about/strategies/social-stories-comic-strips.aspx

Blog post that explains what social stories and comic strip conversations are and how autistic people can use them to improve communication, safety, and self-care.

The Significance of Semantics: Person-First Language: Why It Matters[36]

> www.autistichoya.com/2011/08/significance-of-semantics-person-first.html

> Blog post that discusses the difference between person-first (individual with autism) vs. autism-first (autistic individual) language. It explores the history of the linguistic debate and why it's important.

WTBS 13 Transgender Patients: How to Foster a Safer Emergency Department Environment[37]

> https://emergencymedicinecases.com/transgender-patients-emergency-department

> Blog post, from an emergency medicine doctor, that discusses common issues for transgender people in emergency rooms and explores ways that these environments can be made more transgender friendly.

JOURNAL ARTICLES

Postsecondary Employment Experiences Among Young Adults with an Autism Spectrum Disorder RH: Employment in Young Adults with Autism[38]

> An article that examines employment issues for autistic people.

Race Influences Parent Report of Concerns About Symptoms of Autism Spectrum Disorder[39]

> Academic article about how race plays a role in the recognition of autism symptoms. It specifically investigated whether Black parents reported fewer autism concerns than white parents among a sample of 174 18–40-month-old children.

Reclaiming Travesti Histories[40]

> A fascinating academic article on the impact of Spanish colonization on the expression of gender diversity in Latin America, its impact on modern-day gender diverse people, and the reclamation of the term *travesti*.

The AASPIRE Practice-Based Guidelines for the Inclusion of Autistic Adults in Research as Co-Researchers and Study Participants[41]

Academic article from the Academic Autistic Spectrum Partnership in Research and Education presenting guidelines for the inclusion of autistic individuals as co-researchers and participants in academic research.

The Empire Strikes Back: A Posttranssexual Manifesto[42]

This article is a response to a widely published anti-transgender essay. The author uses this essay to establish the existence of transgender people throughout history and privilege transgender people's perspectives on the "transgender body" over those of cisgender individuals and professionals.

"What's the Point of Having Friends?": Reformulating Notions of the Meaning of Friends and Friendship Among Autistic People[43]

Academic article about autistic people's interpretation and experiences of friendship and how they sometimes differ fundamentally from neurotypical individuals.

Whose Expertise Is It? Evidence for Autistic Adults as Critical Autism Experts[44]

An article based on a study of autistic adults that presents an argument for the inclusion and leadership of autistic adults in research on the subject.

Why Sheldon Cooper Can't be Black: The Visual Rhetoric of Autism and Ethnicity[45]

An article that explains how the concept of autism is constructed in such a way as to preclude people of colour.

BOOKS

All the Weight of Our Dreams: On Living Racialized Autism[46]

Book about the experience of racialized people who are autistic.

Authoring Autism: On Rhetoric and Neurological Queerness[47]

Academic book that defines autism as an identity instead of an impairment. It challenges how autism has been pathologized and criticizes behavioural interventions such as ABA, likening them to gay conversion therapy. She also argues that autistic people are the best equipped to talk about their own experiences of autism.

Call Me Crazy: Stories from the Mad Movement[48]

Book about the history and current status of the Mad Movement. Also tells the author's story of going from a patient to an activist.

Uncomfortable Labels[49]

Insightful and candid memoir from a transgender woman who is gay and autistic.

WEBSITES AND PODCASTS
Aftereffect[50]

Podcast about the long-term impacts on an autistic man whose caregiver was shot by police after they mistook the man's toy truck for a firearm.

Gender Dysphoria & Autism with Aron Janssen MD[51]

Podcast featuring autism and transgender specialist Dr. Aron Janssen. It explores the overlap between these two issues from the viewpoint of a clinician.

JOURNALS, MAGAZINES, AND MEDIA COLLECTIVES
Altogether Autism

http://altogetherautism.org.nz

A New Zealand-based journal on autism.

NOS Magazine

http://nosmag.org

Web magazine with articles by and for autistic folks.

The Aspergian

https://theaspergian.com

Collective of neurodivergent individuals who are cataloging the experience, insights, knowledge, talents, and creative pursuits of autistics.

The Thinking Person's Guide to Autism

www.thinkingautismguide.com

Guide and blog on information for autistic people, professionals, and parents.

ENDNOTES

1   Academic Autistic Spectrum Partnership in Research and Education, n.d.
2   Ashkenazy & Latimer, 2013
3   Ashkenazy & Yergeau, 2013
4   Kerrigan *et al.*, 2015
5   Howard *et al.*, 2010
6   Holton, 2013
7   Sugar, 2013
8   Channel 4, 2009
9   Pellicano, 2018
10 Parker, 2015
11 Quinn & Sullivan, 2018
12 Koetse, 2015
13 Davis, 2006
14 Fonrobert, n.d.
15 Aviv, 2018
16 Burns, 2017
17 Baume, 2016
18 Kurchak, 2018
19 Devita-Raeburn & Spectrum, 2016
20 Pilkington, 2018
21 Butrymowicz, 2017
22 Weiss, 2016
23 Wired Staff, 2001
24 Russo, 2018
25 Payton, 2015

26 Silberman, 2016
27 Benaway, 2018
28 Crow, 2017
29 Williams, 2019
30 Sidney, n.d.
31 Tagonist, 2009
32 Bauer, Winegar, & Waxman, 2016
33 Smith, 2017
34 Schaber, n.d.
35 National Autistic Society, 2018
36 Brown, 2011
37 Ovens, 2017
38 Roux *et al.*, 2014
39 Donohue *et al.*, 2019
40 Campuzano, 2006
41 Nicolaidis *et al.*, 2019
42 Stone, 1992
43 Bertilsdotter Rosqvist, Brownlow, & O'Dell, 2015
44 Gillespie-Lynch *et al.*, 2017
45 Matthews, 2019
46 Brown, Ashkenazy, & Onaiwu, 2017
47 Yergeau, 2018
48 Shimrat, 1997
49 Dale, 2019
50 Quinn, 2018
51 Burke, 2016

Appendix 1: Informed Consent Form

Our names are Noah Adams, Bridget Liang, and Reubs Walsh. We are independent researchers looking at the experience of folks who are both transgender and autistic for a forthcoming book on the topic with Jessica Kingsley Publishers. As we are people who are also transgender and autistic, this topic has a lot of personal meaning to us and we are committed to treating your responses and stories with respect and dignity.

We are asking that you answer a short questionnaire about your experiences of being transgender and autistic. This will help us to get a basic sense of what this community looks like. This questionnaire will take up to 20 minutes to complete, after which we will interview you for approximately one to three hours. Following the interview, you will be eligible for a $100 CAD honorarium. We will also ask you to recruit two other transgender/autistic people, who will be eligible for the same honorarium after completing this interview. This is a recruitment technique known as snowball sampling, and will help us to introduce a random element to our inclusion of participants.

As this is a small community, you may know or have worked with us. Whether or not this is the case, you should not feel pressured to take part in this study, nor will there be any negative effects should you choose not to, or later drop out. Regardless, all responses will be anonymous, unless you request otherwise.

If you have any questions about the study, please contact Noah Adams.

INFORMED CONSENT

We invite you to take part in a study on the experiences of individuals who are transgender and autistic. Your participation is voluntary, does not pay any money, and you may drop out at any time. The information below tells you about any risks or drawbacks that may result, and while your participation probably won't help you, we might learn things that will help improve future research.

WHO WILL BE CONDUCTING THIS RESEARCH?

Noah Adams, MSW
Toronto, Ontario
noah@noahjadams.com

Bridget Liang
Toronto, Ontario
b.jianjian@gmail.com

Reubs Walsh
Amsterdam, Netherlands
Vrije Universiteit
r.j.walsh@vu.nl

STUDY PURPOSE

The purpose of this study is to explore the experiences of adults who identify as transgender and autistic.

WHO CAN PARTICIPATE IN THIS STUDY?

Anyone who self-identifies or is diagnosed as both autistic and transgender, and is 18 years or older.

WHAT WILL YOU BE ASKED TO DO?

You will be asked to take part in an audio-recorded conversation about your experiences as transgender and autistic using your choice of telephone, Skype, or, if possible, in person, at a time and place of your choosing. You will be asked to confirm that you identify and/or are diagnosed as transgender and autistic and provide some basic demographic data (e.g. income, ethnicity, disability). After this you will be asked to discuss your experiences as a person who is both transgender and autistic for between one and three hours. This information will be edited and used to form a chapter of the book and you will receive a draft copy of this chapter and a chance to respond, before publication, with any comments or corrections. You will not receive co-authorship on the resulting publication.

POSSIBLE DISCOMFORTS AND RISKS

There is no physical risk associated with this study and the risk of emotional discomfort is remote. You should also be aware that we will go to great lengths to protect your anonymity unless, of course, you prefer to be identified.

POSSIBLE BENEFITS

On completion of the interview, you will receive an email with the final results of this research, a free copy of the resulting book, and an honorarium of $100 CAD. Your participation will also assist in better understanding this topic and you may also appreciate thinking and speaking about your experiences.

COMPENSATION AND REIMBURSEMENT

Those who complete the interview will receive a $100 CAD honorarium for their participation, as well as a free copy of the resulting book.

CONFIDENTIALITY AND ANONYMITY

All interviews will be audio recorded and saved under password on the researcher's computer. The researcher will type out the audio file, word for word, and save it to their laptop under a password, at which time the audio file will be deleted. On completion of this research, these files will be stored for five years, after which they will be securely deleted.

Your interview will be used to write a single chapter of the book and reported in such a way as to preserve your anonymity. You will be given a chance to select a pseudonym for use in the book, and if you choose not to select one, one will be chosen for you. You will also receive a draft copy of your chapter for review and comment and will be advised about including or excluding information that may identify you. You will be given the option to be identifiable and de-anonymized in the book, if you so choose. Ultimately, confidentiality will be protected to the degree permitted by law and, in most cases, no one but the researchers will see the text or audio files. However, the researchers have a legal duty to report suspected child abuse or neglect, the abuse or neglect of an adult in need of protection, and/or risk or threat of harm to self or others.

PARTICIPATION IS VOLUNTARY

Participation in this study is voluntary. You are free to turn it down or withdraw at any time, subject to the following guidelines. You are also free to skip any questions, pause the interview, or stop completely, at any time, without explanation.

QUESTIONS AND DROPPING OUT

Contact Noah Adams at noah@noahjadams.com if you wish to drop out or have questions. You are free to withdraw your consent until June 30th, after which we will begin the writing process. Dropping out of this study will have no impact on any existing professional or personal relationship with the researchers. During this study, you will be informed of any new information that might affect your decision to remain in it.

CONFLICT OF INTEREST

This research has no sponsor, and while the publication of the resulting book may result in modest royalties, these will be used to pay for the honoraria provided to interviewees.

I have read the details about this study. I have been given a chance to talk about it and my questions have been answered. I hereby consent to take part in this study; however, I know that my participation is voluntary and that I may withdraw at any time.

Participant

Name: . . . .

Signature: . . . .

Date: . . . .

Researcher

Name: . . . .

Signature: . . . .

Date: . . . .

I understand that this interview will be audio recorded and I give consent to do so.

Participant

Name: . . . .

Signature: . . . .

Date: . . . .

Researcher

Name: . . . .

Signature: . . . .

Date: . . . .

I agree to let you directly quote any comments or statements made in any written or audio reports, without seeing the quotes prior to their use, and I understand that my anonymity will be preserved by not attributing them to me.

Participant

Name: . . . .

Signature: . . . .

Date: . . . .

Researcher

Name: . . . .

Signature: . . . .

Date: . . . .

I wish to be identifiable in the resulting publication by Jessica Kingsley Publishers.

Participant

Name: . . . .

Signature: . . . .

Date: . . . .

Researcher

Name: . . . .

Signature: . . . .

Date: . . . .

You will get a copy of this form for your records.

Appendix 2: Interview Questions

1. When did you first know you were autistic?

   a. (Prompt) What was it like "coming out"?

2. When did you first know you were trans/non-cis?

   a. (Prompt) What was it like "coming out"?

   b. (Prompt) How would you describe your gender identity now? How did you reach the terminology/language you use?

3. Do you think autism and gender identity are related?

   a. (If non-binary) Do you feel like your being non-binary is related to being autistic?

4. Do you have a self-identified or diagnosed disability other than autism spectrum?

   a. (Prompt) How does that interact with your autism spectrum?

5. Tell me about your family.

   a. (Prompt) Are they supportive of your gender identity/autism?

   b. (Prompt) Is anyone else in your family autistic/trans?

6. Are you involved in the autism/trans community?

7. Tell me about your experience with healthcare (mental/physical/autism/transgender).

   a. (Prompt) Do you need/receive any accommodations and/or supports?

   b. (Prompt) Does being trans/autistic make your relationship with healthcare more difficult?

8. Do you see your experiences reflected in the media/popular culture?

9. What is your experience with everyday social rules/conventions and those specific to gender?

   a. (Prompt) Do people treat you differently because you're transgender and/or autistic?

10. Do you have anything you want to add?

Appendix 3: Demographic Questions

1. What is your age?

   . . . .

2. What country and city were you born in?

   . . . .

3. What country and city do you presently live in?

   . . . .

4. What pronouns do you use?

   . . . .

5. What sex were you assigned at birth (on your original birth certificate)?[1]

☐ Female

☐ Male

☐ Prefer not to say

☐ Other; please specify:

. . . .

6. Which of the following describes your present gender identity? (Please check all that apply.)[2]

☐ Bi-gender

☐ Boy or Man

☐ Crossdresser

☐ Feel like a boy sometimes

☐ Feel like a girl sometimes

☐ FTM

☐ Genderqueer

☐ Girl or Woman

☐ MTF

☐ T Girl

☐ Trans Boy or Trans Man

☐ Trans Girl or Trans Woman

☐ Two-spirit

☐ Other; please specify:

. . . .

7. Which of the following describes your present sexual orientation? (Please check all that apply.)

☐ Ace spectrum

☐ Bisexual

☐ Gay

☐ Lesbian

☐ Pansexual

☐ Queer

☐ Straight or Heterosexual

☐ Two-spirit

☐ Not sure or Questioning

☐ Other; please specify:

. . . .

8. Are you on the autism spectrum?

    ☐ No

    ☐ Yes

    ☐ I don't know

    ☐ I'd rather not say

    a. What is your specific diagnosis?

        ☐ Asperger's

        ☐ Autism

        ☐ Non-verbal learning disability

        ☐ I don't know

        ☐ I'd rather not say

        ☐ Other; please specify:

        . . . .

    b. Are you formally or self-diagnosed?

        ☐ Formally

        ☐ Self-diagnosed

        ☐ I don't know

☐ I'd rather not say

☐ Other; please specify:

. . . .

9. Please identify and describe your racial/ethnic identity.

. . . .

. . . .

. . . .

10. What is your best estimate of your total income, before taxes and deductions, from all sources in the past 12 months? *Please specify denomination and to the nearest amount you know and/or feel comfortable.*

. . . .

11. At this point, what is the highest level of education you have **completed**?

☐ Did not graduate from high/secondary school

☐ High/secondary school graduate

☐ Some college or trade school

☐ College or trade school graduate

☐ Some university

☐ University – Bachelor's degree

☐ University – Graduate or professional degree

☐ I don't know

☐ I'd rather not say

ENDNOTES

1   Questions 5 and 7 were adapted from the National Transgender Discrimination Survey (Grant *et al.*, 2011).
2   Questions 6 and 11 were adapted from Trans PULSE (Bauer & Scheim, 2015).

References

Academic Autistic Spectrum Partnership in Research and Education. (n.d.). AASPIRE healthcare toolkit: primary care resources for adults on the autism spectrum and their primary care providers. Retrieved from https://autismandhealth.org.

Adams, N., Hitomi, M., & Moody, C. (2017). Varied reports of adult transgender suicidality: synthesizing and describing the peer reviewed and gray literature. *Transgender Health, 2(1)*, 60–75.

Adams, N., Pearce, R., Veale, J., Radix, A., *et al.* (2017). Guidance and ethical considerations for undertaking transgender health research and institutional review boards adjudicating this research. *Transgender Health, 2(1)*, 165–175.

Adler, L. & White, M. (Producers), & Sharman, J. (Director). (1975). *Rocky Horror Picture Show* [Motion picture]. United States: 20th Century Fox.

ArenaNet. (2012). *Guild Wars 2* [Video game]. Bellevue, WA: NCSOFT.

Asante, M. & Davis, A. (1985). Black and white communication: analyzing work place encounters. *Journal of Black Studies, 16(1)*, 77–93.

Ashkenazy, E. & Latimer, M. (eds). (2013). *Navigating College: A Handbook on Self-Advocacy Written for Autistic Students from Autistic Adults*. Washington, DC: Autistic Self Advocacy Network.

Ashkenazy, E. & Yergeau, M. (eds). (2013). *A Handbook for Autistic People: Relationships and Sexuality*. Washington, DC: Autistic Self Advocacy Network.

Asia Pacific Transgender Network. (2017, Oct 8). "Nothing for us without us": Asia Pacific Transgender Network (APTN) insists on trans-led initiatives to serve trans populations in the Asia Pacific region. Retrieved from www.weareaptn.org/2017/10/08/nothing-for-us-without-us-asia-pacific-transgender-network-aptn-insists-on-trans-led-initiatives-to-serve-trans-populations-in-the-asia-pacific-region.

Asperger/Autism Network. (n.d.). Wallet card. Retrieved from www.aane.org/resources/wallet-card.

Auer, M.K., Fuss, J., Hohne, N., Stalla, G.K., & Sievers, C. (2014). Transgender transitioning and change of self-reported sexual orientation. *PLOS One, 9(10)*, 1–11.

Autism Canada. (2017). Sign language or signed speech. Retrieved from https://autismcanada.org/living-with-autism/treatments/non-medical/communication/sign-language.

Autism Society of Alabama. (n.d.). Autism identification card. Retrieved from www.autism-alabama.org/what-is-autism/autism-driver-identification-card.

Autistics For Autistics. (n.d.). Retrieved from https://a4aontario.com/about.

Aviv, R. (2018, Sept 24). Georgia's separate and unequal special-education system. *The New Yorker*. Retrieved from www.newyorker.com/magazine/2018/10/01/georgias-separate-and-unequal-special-education-system.

Bai, D., Yip, B.H.K., Windham, G.C., Sourander, A., *et al.* (2019). Association of genetic and environmental factors with autism in a 5-country cohort. *JAMA Psychiatry, 76(10),* 1035–1043.

Bakan, M.B. (2015). The musicality of stimming: promoting neurodiversity in the ethnomusicology of autism. *MUSICultures, 41(2),* 133–161.

Barahona-Correa, J.B. & Filipe, C.N. (2015). A concise history of Asperger syndrome: reign of a troublesome diagnosis. *Frontiers in Psychology, 6(2024),* 1–7.

Bargiela, S., Steward, R., & Mandy, W. (2016). The experiences of late-diagnosed women with autism spectrum conditions: an investigation of the female autism phenotype. *Journal of Autism and Developmental Disorders, 46(10),* 3281–3294.

Baron-Cohen, S. (2003). *The Essential Difference: Male and Female Brains and the Truth About Autism.* New York, NY: Basic Books.

Baron-Cohen, S., Wheelwright, S., Skinner, R., Martin, J., & Clubley, E. (2002). The autism-spectrum quotient (AQ): evidence from Asperger syndrome/high functioning autism, males and females, scientists and mathematicians. *Journal of Autism and Developmental Disorders, 31(1),* 5–17.

Bauer, G.R. & Scheim, A.I. (2015). Transgender people in Ontario, Canada: statistics from the Trans PULSE Project to inform human rights policy. Retrieved from http://transpulseproject.ca/wp-content/uploads/2015/06/Trans-PULSE-Statistics-Relevant-for-Human-Rights-Policy-June-2015.pdf.

Bauer, S.C., Winegar, J., & Waxman, S. (2016, April 1). How cultural differences affect autism diagnoses [Blog post]. Retrieved from https://blogs.scientificamerican.com/guest-blog/how-cultural-differences-affect-autism-diagnoses.

Baume, M. (2016, Sept 9). How trans players find support from the gaming community. *Vice.* Retrieved from www.vice.com/en_ca/article/8gegvx/how-trans-players-find-support-from-the-gaming-community-58477ff7b003780236751598.

Benaway, G. (2018). When it comes to health care, transphobia persists. *The Globe and Mail.* Retrieved from www.theglobeandmail.com/opinion/article-when-it-comes-to-health-care-transphobia-persists.

Benford, P. & Standen, P.J. (2011). The use of email-facilitated interviewing with higher functioning autistic people participating in a grounded theory study. *International Journal of Social Research Methodology, 14(5),* 353–368.

Bertilsdotter Rosqvist, H., Brownlow, C., & O'Dell, L. (2015). "What's the point of having friends?": reformulating notions of the meaning of friends and friendship among autistic people. *Disability Studies Quarterly, 35(4).* Retrieved from http://dsq-sds.org/article/view/3254/4109.

BioWare Austin. (2011). *Star Wars: The Old Republic* [Video game]. Edmonton, Canada: Electronic Arts.

Blizzard Entertainment. (2004). *World of Warcraft* [Video game]. Irvine, CA: Blizzard Entertainment.

Bonvillian, J.D., Nelson, K.E., & Rhyne, J.M. (1981). Sign language and autism. *Journal of Autism and Developmental Disorders, 11(1)*, 125–137.

Bouman, W.P., Schwend, A.S., Motmans, J., Smiley, A., *et al.* (2017). Language and trans health. *International Journal of Transgenderism, 18(1)*, 1–6.

Bourns, A. (2016). *Guidelines and Protocols for Hormone Therapy and Primary Health Care for Trans Clients*. Toronto: Sherbourne Health Centre. Retrieved from http://sherbourne.on.ca/wp-content/uploads/2014/02/Guidelines-and-Protocols-for-Comprehensive-Primary-Care-for-Trans-Clients-2015.pdf.

Brill, S.A. (2016). *The Transgender Teen: A Handbook for Parents and Professionals Supporting Transgender and Non-Binary Teens*. New Jersey, NJ: Cleis Press.

Brown, L.X.Z. (2011, Aug 4). The significance of semantics: person-first language: why it matters [Blog post]. Retrieved from www.autistichoya.com/2011/08/significance-of-semantics-person-first.html.

Brown, L.X.Z., Ashkenazy, C., & Onaiwu, M.G. (2017). *All the Weight of Our Dreams: On Living Racialized Autism*. Lincoln, NE: DragonBee Press.

Burke, C. (2016, Jan 26). *Gender Dysphoria & Autism with Aron Janssen MD* [Audio podcast]. Retrieved from http://ackerman.podbean.com/e/the-ackerman-podcast-22-gender-dysphoria-autism-with-aron-janssen-md.

Burns, K. (2017, April 24). How our society harms trans people who are also autistic. *The Establishment*. Retrieved from https://medium.com/the-establishment/how-our-society-harms-trans-people-with-autism-9766edc6553d.

Butrymowicz, S. (2017, Nov 11). Low academic expectations and poor support for special education students are "hurting their future." *The Hechinger Report*. Retrieved from https://hechingerreport.org/low-academic-expectations-poor-support-special-education-students-hurting-future.

Camp Kennebec. (n.d.). Retrieved from www.campkennebec.com.

Campuzano, G. (2006). Reclaiming travesti histories. *IDS Bulletin, 37(5)*, 34–39.

Carruthers, S., Kinnaird, E., Rudra, A., Smith, P., *et al.* (2018). A cross-cultural study of autistic traits across India, Japan and the UK. *Molecular Autism, 9(52)*, 1–10.

Cassidy, S. & Rodgers, J. (2017). Understanding and prevention of suicide in autism. *The Lancet, 4(6)*. Retrieved from www.thelancet.com/journals/lanpsy/article/PIIS2215-0366(17)30162-1/fulltext.

Cendrowski, M. (Director). (2007). *The Big Bang Theory* [Television series]. C. Lorre, S. Molaro, B. Prady, & E. Kaplan (Producers). Los Angeles, CA: Warner Bros. Television.

Centre for Addiction and Mental Health. (n.d.). Gender identity clinic (adult). Retrieved from www.camh.ca/en/your-care/programs-and-services/gender-identity-clinic-adult.

Channel 4. (2009). *The Boy Who Was Born a Girl*. Retrieved from www.youtube.com/watch?v=SLINZ5iA8nY.

Channel 4. (n.d.). *Genderquake*. Retrieved from www.channel4.com/programmes/genderquake.

Charlton, J.I. (2000). *Nothing About Us Without Us: Disability Oppression and Empowerment*. Los Angeles, CA: University of California Press.

Chen, R. (2017, Oct 10). I'm a light-skinned Chinese woman, and I experience pretty privilege. *Teen Vogue*. Retrieved from www.teenvogue.com/story/pretty-privilege-and-colorism-as-a-fair-skinned-chinese-woman.

Chisolm-Straker, M., Jardine, L., Bennouna, C., Morency-Brassard, N., *et al.* (2017, Feb 1). Transgender and gender nonconforming in emergency departments: a qualitative report of patient experiences. *Transgender Health, 2(1)*. Retrieved from www.liebertpub.com/doi/full/10.1089/trgh.2016.0026.

Coleman, E., Bockting, W., Botzer, M., Cohen-Kettenis, P., *et al.* (2012). Standards of care for the health of transsexual, transgender, and gender-nonconforming people, version 7. *International Journal of Transgenderism, 13(4)*, 165–232.

Craig, F., Margari, F., Legrottaglie, A.R., Palumbi, R., de Giambattista, C., & Margari, L. (2016). A review of executive function deficits in autism spectrum disorder and attention-deficit/hyperactivity disorder. *Neuropsychiatric Disease and Treatment, 12*, 1191–1202.

Crow, M. (2017, Nov 21). Anarchism: in the conversations of neurodiversity [Blog post]. Retrieved from https://maxxcrow.wordpress.com/2017/12/07/anarchism-in-the-conversations-of-neurodiversity.

Cuil Press. (n.d.). Kalonymus ben Kalonymus: transgender history gets a pat on the head. Retrieved from www.cuilpress.com/2017/10/16/kalonymus-ben-kalonymus-transgender-history.

Dale, K.D. (2019). *Uncomfortable Labels*. London: Jessica Kingsley Publishers.

Daniel, A. (2017). *Dreadnought: Nemesis*. New York, NY: Diversion Publishing.

Davis, J. (2006, Nov 11). Face blind. *Wired*. Retrieved from www.wired.com/2006/11/blind.

Davis, N. (2019, Feb 26). Trans patients in England face "soul destroying" wait for treatment. *The Guardian*. Retrieved from www.theguardian.com/society/2019/feb/26/trans-patients-in-england-face-soul-destroying-wait-for-treatment.

Daybreak Game Company. (2010). *Clone Wars Adventures* [Video game]. San Diego, CA: Sony Online Entertainment.

de Marchena, A.B., Eigsti, I-M., & Yerys, B.E. (2015). Brief report: generalization weaknesses in verbally fluent children and adolescents with autism spectrum disorder. *Journal of Autism and Developmental Disorders, 45(10)*, 3370–3376.

Demetriou, E.A., Lampit, A., Quintana, D.S., Naismith, S.L., *et al.* (2017). Autism spectrum disorders: a meta-analysis of executive function. *Molecular Psychiatry, 23*, 1198–1204.

Dempsey, A. (2018, May 14). Inside the life of Alek Minassian, the Toronto van rampage suspect no one thought capable of murder. *The Hamilton Spectator*. Retrieved from www.thespec.com/news-story/8605039-inside-the-life-of-alek-minassian-the-toronto-van-rampage-suspect-no-one-thought-capable-of-murder.

Devita-Raeburn, E. & Spectrum. (2016, Aug 11). Is the most common therapy for autism cruel? *The Atlantic*. Retrieved from www.theatlantic.com/health/archive/2016/08/aba-autism-controversy/495272.

Dimbort, D., Heid, M.D., DeMartini, F., & Lawrence, R. (Producers), & Naess, P. (Director). (2005). *Mozart and the Whale* [Motion picture]. United States: Millennium Films.

Donohue, M.R., Childs, A.W., Richards, M., & Robins, D.L. (2019). Race influences parent report of concerns about symptoms of autism spectrum disorder. *Autism, 23(1)*, 100–111.

Draeper, J. (2017, May 27). Autism diagnosis "could be reduced under NHS plan." *BBC News*. Retrieved from www.bbc.com/news/health-40058482.

Dym, B., Brubaker, J., & Fiesler, C. (2018). "They're all trans Sharon": authoring gender in video game fan fiction. *Game Studies, 18(3)*. Retrieved from http://gamestudies.org/1803/articles/brubaker_dym_fiesler.

Egale Canadian Human Rights Trust. (n.d.). Egale youth services. Retrieved from https://egale.ca/youthservices.

Ehrensaft, D., Giammattei, S.V., Storck, K., Tishelman, A.C., & Keo-Meier, C. (2018). Prepubertal social gender transitions: what we know; what we can learn—a view from a gender affirmative lens. *International Journal of Transgenderism, 19(2)*, 251–268.

Eldred-Cohen, C. (2018, Aug 12). How Satoshi Tajiri's autism helped create Pokemon. *The Art of Autism*. Retrieved from https://the-art-of-autism.com/how-satoshi-tajiris-autism-helped-create-pokemon.

Ellis, R. (2016, Feb 7). Transgender man with Asperger's killed by Mesa, Arizona, police. *CNN*. Retrieved from www.cnn.com/2016/02/06/us/transgender-man-with-aspergers-killed/index.html.

Faraday, C. (2014). *For lack of a better word: neo-identities in non-cisgender, non-straight communities on Tumblr* (Master's thesis). Ryerson University, Toronto.

Ferguson, S. & Saines, E.G. (Producers), & Jackson, M. (Director). (2010). *Temple Grandin* [Motion picture]. United States: HBO Films.

Fletcher-Watson, S. (2016, Aug 15). Autistic person, or person with autism? [Blog post]. Retrieved from https://dart.ed.ac.uk/autism-language.

Fonrobert, C.E. (n.d.). Gender identity in Halakhic discourse. *Jewish Women's Archive*. Retrieved from https://jwa.org/encyclopedia/article/gender-identity-in-halakhic-discourse.

FTM London. (n.d.). Retrieved from https://ftmlondon.net.

Gammicchia, C. & Johnson, C. (2014, April). Autism: information for domestic violence and sexual assault counsellors. Retrieved from www.autism-society.org/wp-content/uploads/2014/04/Domestic_Violence___Sexual_Assault_Counsellors.pdf.

Gargaro, B.A., Rinehart, N.J., Bradshaw, J.L., Tonge, B.J., & Sheppard, D.M. (2011). Autism and ADHD: how far have we come in the comorbidity debate? *Neuroscience & Biobehavioral Reviews, 35(5)*, 1081–1088.

Gender Infinity Conference. (n.d.). Retrieved from http://genderinfinityconference.org.

Genderqueer Chicago. (n.d.). Retrieved from www.genderqueerchicago.org.

George, R. & Stokes, M.A. (2018). Sexual orientation in autism spectrum disorder. *Autism Research, 11(1)*, 133–141.

Gillespie-Lynch, K., Kapp, S.K., Brooks, P.J., Pickens, J., & Schwartzman, B. (2017). Whose expertise is it? Evidence for autistic adults as critical autism experts. *Frontiers in Psychology, 8(438)*, 1–14.

Gordon, S. (Director). (2017). *Atypical* [Television series]. R. Rashid, S. Gordon, & M. Rohlich (Producers). Los Angeles, CA: Netflix.

Gourdine, R.M., Baffour, T.D., & Teasley, M. (2011). Autism and the African American community. *Social Work and Public Health, 26(4)*, 454–470.

Graffeo, D., Brown, E., & Freeman, Z. (2019, Jan 10). Trans healthcare activism in Ontario. *Canadian Gay and Lesbian Archive*. Retrieved from http://digitalcollections.clga.ca/exhibits/show/trans-surgery-activism-ontario/transhealthactivismproject.

Grant, J.M., Mottet, L.A., Tanis, J., Harrison, J., Herman, J.L., & Keisling, M. (2011). *Injustice at Every Turn: A Report of the National Transgender Discrimination Survey*. Washington, DC: National Center for Transgender Equality and National Gay and Lesbian Task Force.

Halberstam, J. (1998). *Female Masculinity*. Durham, NC: Duke University Press.

Hendricks, D. (2010). Employment and adults with autism spectrum disorders: challenges and strategies for success. *Journal of Vocational Rehabilitation, 32(2)*, 125–134.

Hitomi, M. (2018). *In transition: analyzing shifting and competing Anglophone discourses impacting Canadian trans people* (Master's thesis). University of Saskatchewan, Saskatoon.

Holton, A.E. (2013). What's wrong with Max? Parenthood and the portrayal of autism spectrum disorders. *Journal of Communication Inquiry, 37(1)*, 45–63.

Howard, R., Grazer, B., Katims, J., Trilling, L., Watson, S., & Nevins, D. (Executive producers). (2010). *Parenthood* [Television series]. United States: NBC Universal Television.

Howlin, P., Alcock, J., & Burkin, C. (2005). An 8 year follow-up of a specialist supported employment service for high-ability adults with autism or Asperger syndrome. *Autism, 9(5)*, 533–549.

Human Rights Campaign. (n.d.). Violence against the transgender community in 2018 [Blog post]. Retrieved from www.hrc.org/resources/violence-against-the-transgender-community-in-2018.

Jackson, K. (2013, July 8). The mad movement, Marxism, and mad activism today. *The Socialist Worker*. Retrieved from www.socialist.ca/node/1825.

Jacobs, L.A., Rachlin, K., Erickson-Schroth, L., & Janssen, A. (2014). Gender dysphoria and co-occurring autism spectrum disorders: review, case examples, and treatment considerations. *LGBT Health, 1(4)*, 277–82.

James, S.E., Herman, J.L., Rankin, S., Keisling, M., Mottet, L., & Anafi, M. (2016). *The Report of the 2015 U.S. Transgender Survey*. Washington, DC: National Center for Transgender Equality.

Janssen, A., Huang, H., & Duncan, C. (2016). Gender variance among youth with autism spectrum disorders: a retrospective chart review. *Transgender Health, 1(1)*, 63–68.

Johnson, M. (Producer), & Levinson, B. (Director). (1988). *Rain Man* [Motion picture]. United States: MGM/UA Communications Company.

Jones, R.M., Wheelwright, S., Farrell, K., Martin, E., *et al.* (2012). Brief report: female-to-male transsexual people and autistic traits. *Journal of Autism and Developmental Disorders, 42(2)*, 301–306.

Katz-Wise, S.L., Reisner, S.L., White Hughto, J., & Keo-Meier, C.L. (2016). Differences in sexual orientation diversity and sexual fluidity in attractions among gender minority adults in Massachusetts. *The Journal of Sex Research, 53(1)*, 74–84.

Keen, D., Webster, A., & Ridley, G. (2016). How well are children with autism spectrum disorder doing academically at school? An overview of the literature. *Autism, 20(3)*, 276–294.

Keo-Meier, C. (n.d.). Research. Retrieved from http://coltkeo-meier.com/research.

Kerrigan, E., Carlyle, S., & Mettam, A. (Writers),Clarke-Jervoise, S. (Producer), & Walker, P. (Director). (2015). *Boy Meets Girl* [Television series]. Newcastle upon Tyne, Tyne and Wear, UK: Endemol UK.

Knutson, D., Koch, J.M., Arthur, T., Mitchell, A., & Martyr, M.A. (2016). "Trans broken arm": health care stories from transgender people in rural areas. *Journal of Research on Women and Gender, 7*, 30–46.

Koetse, M. (2015, Aug 14). Behind the spotlights of transgender China. *What's on Weibo*. Retrieved from www.whatsonweibo.com/behind-the-spotlights-of-transgender-china.

Kukla, R.E. (2006). Terms for gender diversity in classical Jewish texts. *TransTorah*. Retrieved from www.transtorah.org/PDFs/Classical_Jewish_Terms_for_Gender_Diversity.pdf.

Kumitz, D. (2016). Nothing about us without us: self-representation in social protection in Southern Africa. *Global Social Policy: An Interdisciplinary Journal of Public Policy and Social Development, 16(2)*, 215–217.

Kupferstein, H. (2018). Evidence of increased PTSD symptoms in autistics exposed to applied behavior analysis. *Advances in Autism, 4(1)*, 19–29.

Kurchak, S. (2018, Feb 22). Imaging a fuller spectrum of autism on TV. *Pacific Standard*. Retrieved from https://psmag.com/social-justice/autistic-license.

Lee, J. (2015, Jul 14). Chokeholds, brain injuries, beatings: when school cops go bad. *Mother Jones*. Retrieved from www.motherjones.com/politics/2015/07/police-school-resource-officers-k-12-misconduct-violence.

Levenson, E. (2017, April 12). North Miami police officer charges with shooting unarmed caretaker. *CNN*. Retrieved from www.cnn.com/2017/04/12/us/north-miami-police-arrest-shooting/index.html.

Lime Connect. (2018, Mar 22). Leading perspectives on disability: a Q&A with Dr. Stephen Shore [Blog post]. Retrieved from www.limeconnect.com/opportunities_news/detail/leading-perspectives-on-disability-a-qa-with-dr-stephen-shore.

Lorenz, T., Frischling, C., Cuadros, R., & Heinitz, K. (2016). Autism and overcoming job barriers: comparing job-related barriers and possible solutions in and outside of autism-specific employment. *PLoS ONE, 11(1)*, 1–19.

Maddox, L.A. (2016). "His wrists were too small": school resource officers and the over-criminalization of America's students. *University of Miami Race & Social Justice Law Review, 6(1)*, 193–216.

Mandell, D.S., Ittenbach, R.F., Levy, S.E., & Pinto-Martin, J.A. (2007). Disparities in diagnoses received prior to a diagnosis of autism spectrum disorder. *Journal of Autism and Developmental Disorders, 37(9)*, 1795–1802.

Mann, A.R. (2013). *The experiences of mothers of children with autism in Jamaica: an exploratory study of their journey* (Unpublished doctoral dissertation). University of South Florida, Tampa, FL. Retrieved from http://scholarcommons.usf.edu/etd/4722.

Matthews, M. (2019). Why Sheldon Cooper can't be Black: the visual rhetoric of autism and ethnicity. *Journal of Literacy & Cultural Disability Studies, 13(1)*, 57–74.

Maxis. (2000). *The Sims* [Video game]. Walnut Creek, CA: Electronic Arts.

McWilliams, A.T. (2018, Jul 25). Sorry to bother you, Black Americans and the power and peril of code-switching. *The Guardian*. Retrieved from www.theguardian.com/film/2018/jul/25/sorry-to-bother-you-white-voice-code-switching.

Meier, S.C., Pardo, S.T., Labuski, C., & Babcock, J. (2013). Measures of clinical health among female-to-male transgender persons as a function of sexual orientation. *Archives of Sexual Behavior, 42(3)*, 463–474.

Meier, S.L.C., Fitzgerald, K.M., Pardo, S.T., & Babcock, J. (2011). The effects of hormonal gender affirmation treatment on mental health in female-to-male transsexuals. *Journal of Gay & Lesbian Mental Health, (15)3*, 281–299.

Mezzofiore, G. (2018, April 25). The Toronto suspect apparently posted about an "incel rebellion." Here's what that means. *CNN World*. Retrieved from https://edition.cnn.com/2018/04/25/us/incel-rebellion-alek-minassian-toronto-attack-trnd/index.html.

Monsebraaten, L. (2018, April 26). "We're not a violent group of people": ex-classmate of Alek Minassian speaks out about autism. *Toronto Star*. Retrieved from www.thestar.com/news/gta/2018/04/26/were-not-a-violent-group-of-people-ex-classmate-of-alek-minassian-speaks-out-about-autism.html.

Morgan, G. (2013, Mar 29). NYPDs "stop and frisk" policy angers LGBT advocacy groups. *Huffpost*. Retrieved from www.huffingtonpost.ca/2013/03/29/nypd-stop-and-frisk-lgbt-groups-_n_2979135.html.

Moyer, M.W. (2019). When autistic people commit sexual crimes. *Spectrum*. Retrieved from www.spectrumnews.org/features/deep-dive/when-autistic-people-commit-sexual-crimes.

Myeong-hong, S., Seung-yeop, L., & Chang-hwan, S. (Producers), & Yoon-cheol, J. (Director). (2005). *Marathon* [Motion picture]. South Korea: Showbox.

National Autistic Society. (2018, July). Social stories and comic strip conversations [Blog post]. Retrieved from www.autism.org.uk/about/strategies/social-stories-comic-strips.aspx.

National Sexual Violence Resource Center (2018). *Responding to Survivors with Autism Spectrum Disorders: An Overview for Sexual Assault Advocates*. Harrisburg, PA: National Sexual Violence Resource Center. Retrieved from www.nsvrc.org/sites/default/files/publications/2018-10/Survivors%20with%20Autism%20Spectrum%20DisordersFINAL508.pdf.

Newport, J. & Newport, M. (2002). *Autism-Asperger's & Sexuality: Puberty and Beyond*. Arlington, TX: Future Horizons.

Nicolaidis, C., Raymaker, D., Kapp, S.K., Baggs, A., *et al.* (2019). The AASPIRE practice-based guidelines for the inclusion of autistic adults in research as co-researchers and study participants. *Autism, 23(8),* 2007–2019.

Nobili, A., Glazebrook, C., Bouman, W.P., Glidden, D., *et al.* (2018). Autistic traits in treatment-seeking transgender adults. *Journal of Autism and Developmental Disorders, 48(12),* 3984–3994.

Ontario Ministry of Children, Community and Social Services. (n.d.). Ontario Autism Program. Retrieved from www.children.gov.on.ca/htdocs/English/specialneeds/autism/ontario-autism-program.aspx.

Ovens, H. (2017, July 17). WTBS 13 transgender patients: how to foster a safer emergency department environment [Blog post]. Retrieved from https://emergencymedicinecases.com/transgender-patients-emergency-department.

Pacific AIDS Network. (n.d.). Nothing about us without us. Retrieved from https://pacificaidsnetwork.org/resources-2/advocacy-policy-public-health/nothing-us-without-us-principles.

Paramo, M. (2016, Oct 10). Life as a homoromantic asexual. *The Queerness.* Retrieved from https://thequeerness.com/2016/10/10/life-as-a-homoromantic-asexual.

Parker, S. (2015, April 6). Autistic and queer: coming out on the spectrum. *AfterEllen.* Retrieved from www.afterellen.com/people/424935-autistic-queer-coming-spectrum.

Payton, N. (2015, Jul 9). The dangers of trans broken arm syndrome. *PinkNews.* Retrieved from www.pinknews.co.uk/2015/07/09/feature-the-dangers-of-trans-broken-arm-syndrome.

Pellicano, L. (2018, April 10). Autism advocacy and research misses the mark if autistic people are left out. *The Conversation.* Retrieved from https://theconversation.com/autism-advocacy-and-research-misses-the-mark-if-autistic-people-are-left-out-94404.

Perry, B. & Dyck, D.R. (2014). "I don't know where it is safe": trans women's experience of violence. *Critical Criminology, 1(22),* 49–63.

Philadelphia Transgender Wellness Conference. (n.d.). Retrieved from www.mazzonicenter.org/trans-wellness.

Pilkington, E. (2018, Nov 16). "It's torture": critics step up bid to stop school using electric shocks on children. *The Guardian.* Retrieved from www.theguardian.com/us-news/2018/nov/16/judge-rotenberg-center-massachusetts-electric-shocks.

Qalonymous ben Qalonymous ben Me'ir & Habermann, A.M. (1956). *Even Bohan.* Tel Aviv, Israel: Mahbarot le-sifrut.

Quinn, A. (2018, June 18). *Aftereffect* [Audio podcast]. Retrieved from https://www.nycstudios.org/podcasts/aftereffect.

Quinn, A. & Sullivan, K. (2018, July 7). Autistic New Yorkers share their stim-toy stories with "Aftereffect." *NPR.* Retrieved from www.npr.org/sections/health-shots/2018/07/07/625756385/autistic-new-yorkers-share-their-stim-toy-stories-with-aftereffect.

Ramirez, R. (2018, Aug 31). It's a cultural moment for Asian representation—as long as you're light skinned. *Huffpost Personal.* Retrieved from www.huffpost.com/entry/darker-skinned-asians-crazy-rich-asians_n_5b881151e4b0511d b3d5b744.

Re:searching for LGBTQ2S+ Health. (n.d.). Two-spirit community. Retrieved from https://lgbtqhealth.ca/community/two-spirit.php.

Richa, S., Fahed, M., Khoury, E., & Mishara, B. (2014). Suicide in autism spectrum disorders. *Archives of Suicide Research, 18(4)*, 327–339.

Ringo, A. (2013, Aug 9). Understanding deafness: not everyone wants to be "fixed." *The Atlantic*. Retrieved from www.theatlantic.com/health/archive/2013/08/understanding-deafness-not-everyone-wants-to-be-fixed/278527.

Robinson, J.E. (2007). *Look Me in the Eye: My Life with Asperger's*. New York, NY: Three Rivers Press.

Roddenberry, G. (Executive Producer). (1966). *Star Trek: The Original Series* [Television series]. United States: Paramount Television.

Roux, A.M., Shattuck, P.T., Cooper, B.P., Anderson, K.A., Wagner, M., & Narendorf, S.C. (2014). Postsecondary employment experiences among young adults with an autism spectrum disorder RH: employment in young adults with autism. *Journal of the American Academy of Child & Adolescent Psychiatry, 52(9)*, 931–939. Retrieved from https://www.ncbi.nlm.nih.gov/pmc/articles/PMC3753691.

Rowe, W. (2009). *Auditioning for care: transsexual men accessing health care* (Master's thesis). McMaster University, Hamilton.

Russo, F. (2018, Feb 21). The costs of camouflaging autism. *Spectrum News*. Retrieved from www.spectrumnews.org/features/deep-dive/costs-camouflaging-autism.

Saban, H., Casentini, B., Bowen, M., & Godfrey, W. (Producers), & Israelite, D. (Director). (2017). *Power Rangers* [Motion picture]. United States: Lionsgate.

Sandin, S., Lichtenstein, P., Kuja-Halkola, R., Hultman, C., Larsson, H., & Reichenberg, A. (2017). The heritability of autism spectrum disorder. *JAMA, 318(12)*, 1182–1184.

Sarrett, J. (2017). Interviews, disclosures, and misperceptions: autistic adults' perspectives on employment related challenges. *Disability Studies Quarterly, 37(2)*. Retrieved from http://dsq-sds.org/article/view/5524/4652.

Schaber, A. (n.d.). *Neurowonderful* [Video blog]. Retrieved from www.youtube.com/channel/UC9Bk0GbW8xgvTgQlheNG5uw.

Schnurr, R. (1999). *Asperger's Huh? A Child's Perspective*. Ottawa, ON: Anisor Publishers.

Schuyler, L., Stohn, S., & Yorke, B. (Executive producers). (2002). *Degrassi: The Next Generation* [Television series]. United States: Program Partners.

Sevlever, M., Roth, M.E., & Gillis, J.M. (2013). Sexual abuse and offending in autism spectrum disorders. *Sexuality and Disability, 31(2)*, 189–200.

Sherbourne Health Centre. (n.d.). Retrieved from https://sherbourne.on.ca.

Shimrat, I. (1997). *Call Me Crazy: Stories from the Mad Movement*. Vancouver, BC: Press Gang Publishers.

Shore, D. & DePaul, S. (Director). (2017). *The Good Doctor* [Television series]. D. Shore, S. Gordon, D.K. Daniel, E. Gunn, D. Kim, S. Lee., M. Listo, & T.LM. Moran (Producers). Vancouver, BC: Sony Pictures Television.

Sidney, H. (n.d.). Exploring non-binary identity theory in the age of the internet or why Tumblr might be right about something for once. [Blog post]. Retrieved from www.oxbowschool.org/assets/gallery/os36-final-projects/docs/sidney-h-os36paper.pdf.

Silberman, S. (2016, May 17). The invisibility of Black autism. *Undark*. Retrieved from https://undark.org/article/invisibility-Black-autism/?fbclid=IwAR05V o0aynvaZozZRfriXxD5k19u41dPblGtcCUWskMYBgHbo9L-BoqRMnU.

Smith, L.T. (1999). *Decolonizing Methodologies: Research and Indigenous Populations*. London, UK: Zed Books.

Smith, T. (2017, May 11). It doesn't have to be this hard [Blog post]. Retrieved from https://tragicgenderstory.com/2017/05/11/it-doesnt-have-to-be-this-hard.

Standifer, S. (2011a). Fact sheet on autism employment. Retrieved from http:// apse.org/wp-content/uploads/docs/AutismEmployment.pdf.

Standifer, S. (2011b). Current trends in autism employment [Power Point slides]. Retrieved from https://www.apse.org/wp-content/uploads/docs/Autism%20 Current%20Trends%20Handouts.pdf

Stone, S. (1992). The empire strikes back: a posttranssexual manifesto. *Camera Obscura, 10(2)*, 150–176.

Strang, J. (2018, Nov 27). Why we need to respect sexual orientation, gender diversity in autism. *Spectrum*, 1–4.

Strang, J.F., Meagher, H., Kenworthy, L., de Vries, A.L.C., *et al.* (2018a). Initial clinical guidelines for co-occurring autism spectrum disorder and gender dysphoria or incongruence in adolescents. *Journal of Clinical Child & Adolescent Psychology, 47(1)*, 105–115.

Strang, J.F., Powers, M.D., Knauss, M., Sibarium, E., *et al.* (2018b). "They thought it was an obsession": trajectories and perspectives of autistic transgender and gender-diverse adolescents. *Journal of Autism and Developmental Disorders, 48(12)*, 4039–4055.

Substance Abuse and Mental Health Services Administration. (2014). *A Treatment Improvement Protocol: Improving Cultural Competence*. Rockville, MD: Substance Abuse and Mental Health Services Administration.

Sugar, R. (Director). (2013). *Steven Universe* [Television series]. R. Sugar, I. Jones-Quartey, & K. Morris (Producers). Los Angeles, CA: Warner Bros. Television.

Supporting Our Youth. (n.d). Trans fusion crew. Retrieved from https:// soytoronto.com/programs/trans-fusion-crew.

Tagonist, A. (2009). Fuck you and your fucking thesis: why I will not participate in trans studies [Blog post]. Retrieved from https://tagonist.livejournal. com/199563.html#/199563.html.

Tannenbaum, N.K. (Producer). (2013). *Orange Is the New Black* [Television series]. United States: Lionsgate.

The 519. (n.d). Meal Trans. Retrieved from www.the519.org/programs/meal-trans.

The 519 Community Centre. (n.d.). Retrieved from www.the519.org.

The Williams Institute. (2015). *Discrimination and Harassment by Law Enforcement Officers in the LGBT Community*. Los Angeles, CA: Christy Mallory, Amira Hasenbush, & Brad Sears.

The Williams Institute. (2016, Oct). *Race and Ethnicity of Adults who Identify as Transgender in the United States*. Los Angeles, CA: A.R. Flores, T.N.T. Brown, & J.L. Herman.

The Williams Institute. (2018). *Transgender Students in Higher Education*. Los Angeles, CA: Abbie G. Goldberg.

Thiessen, J., Wootton, J., Miller, J., Stuby, T., Lu, D., & Myhre, M. (Directors). (2010). *My Little Pony: Friendship is Magic* [Television series]. D. Cody & S. Wall (Producers). Vancouver, BC: Hasbro Studios.

Thom, K.C. (2016, April 15). Sociopaths, borderlines, and psychotics: 3 mental illnesses we must stop hating on. *Everyday Feminism.* Retrieved from https://everydayfeminism.com/2016/04/mental-illnesses-stop-hating-on.

TransBareAll. (n.d.). Retrieved from https://transbareall.co.uk.

Voss, P., Thomas, M.E., Cisneros-Franco, J.M., & Villers-Sidani, E. (2017). Dynamic brains and the changing rules of neuroplasticity: implications for learning and recovery. *Frontiers in Psychology, 8(1647),* 1–11.

Vrangalova, Z. (2018, June 25). Research shows many trans folks' sexual attractions change after transition. *Them.* Retrieved from www.them.us/story/sexual-attraction-after-transition.

Weiss, J.A. & Fardella, M.A. (2018). Victimization and perpetration experiences of adults with autism. *Frontiers in Psychiatry, 9(203),* 1–10.

Weiss, S. (2016, April 21). Meet the people being left out of mainstream conversations about autism. *Complex.* Retrieved from www.complex.com/life/2016/04/autism-women-poc.

White, B. (2016, Nov 15). The link between autism and trans identity. *The Atlantic.* Retrieved from www.theatlantic.com/health/archive/2016/11/the-link-between-autism-and-trans-identity/507509.

Williams, R.A. (2019, July 20). Being nonbinary has nothing to do with looking nonbinary [Blog post]. Retrieved from https://medium.com/@transphilosophr/being-nonbinary-has-nothing-to-do-with-looking-nonbinary-bef864483a43.

Winter, S. (2006). Thai transgenders in focus: demographics, transitions, and identities. *International Journal of Transgenderism, 9(1),* 15–27.

Wired Staff. (2001, Dec 1). Take the autism test. *Wired.* Retrieved from www.wired.com/2001/12/aqtest.

Withers, A.J. (n.d.). What kind of an operation is this? An illustrated guide to the CAMH gender identity clinic [Blog post]. Retrieved from https://stillmyrevolution.files.wordpress.com/2014/01/wht-kind-of-operation-is-this.pdf.

World Professional Association for Transgender Health. (n.d.). Retrieved from www.wpath.org.

Xtra. (2017, Nov 11). This group for autistic LGBT people is creating new conversations in Toronto. *Xtra.* Retrieved from www.dailyxtra.com/this-group-for-autistic-lgbt-people-is-creating-new-conversations-in-toronto-81019.

Yergeau, M. (2018). *Authoring Autism: On Rhetoric and Neurological Queerness.* Durham, NC: Duke University Press.

Subject Index

Author Index